Language *matters*

Language matters

A guide to everyday questions about language

Donna Jo Napoli

Vera Lee-Schoenfeld

OXFORD
UNIVERSITY PRESS

2010

OXFORD
UNIVERSITY PRESS

Oxford   New York
Auckland   Bangkok   Buenos Aires   Cape Town   Chennai
Dar es Salaam   Delhi   Hong Kong   Istanbul   Karachi   Kolkata
Kuala Lumpur   Madrid   Melbourne   Mexico City   Mumbai   Nairobi
São Paulo   Shanghai   Taipei   Tokyo   Toronto

Copyright © 2010 by Oxford University Press, Inc.

Published by Oxford University Press, Inc.
198 Madison Avenue, New York, New York 10016

www.oup.com

Library of Congress Cataloging-in-Publication Data
Napoli, Donna Jo, 1948–
Language matters: a guide to everyday questions about language /
Donna Jo Napoli & Vera Lee-Schoenfeld. — 2nd ed.
    p.   cm.
Includes index.
ISBN 978-0-19-973571-6
1. Language and languages—Miscellanea.   I. Lee-Schoenfeld, Vera.
II. Title.
P107.N37 2010
400—dc22   2009028147

The illustrations appearing on page 163 are from *The World's Writing Systems*,
edited by Peter T. Daniels and William Bright. Copyright 1996 by Oxford University
Press, Inc. Used by permission.

Printed in the United States of America
on acid-free paper

Preface

This book has two authors, one who's been teaching linguistics since 1973, and another who's been teaching languages and linguistics since 1998. Journalists, friends, and people we just happen to have conversations with approach us in that role with questions—ranging all over the board—that often reveal misconceptions about language. We use language in most of our daily interactions with other people, so the types of questions that can arise are at least as varied as the types of situations in which we use language. Here are some examples:

How can we stop our children from using bad grammar?
Why don't we reform English spelling so that the words will
    be spelled exactly as we all say them?
Why are some languages so much harder to speak than
    others?

The first question is problematic because the whole notion of good versus bad grammar is problematic. How do we decide whose grammar is good and whose is not? Language changes from one generation to the next, no matter what, and change is simply that—neither improvement nor deterioration; it is merely change. The second question is based on the assumption that we all pronounce words in the same way. Even within the United States that is false, but certainly, when we look at Canada, England, India,

Australia, Nigeria, and other countries where English is one of the national languages, the falsity of that assumption is obvious. The third question is based on another false assumption. So far as we know, hearing children around the world acquire the spoken language of the people around them with equal ease, and deaf children around the world who are exposed to a sign language acquire that sign language with equal ease. Therefore, it may not make sense to think about languages as being inherently difficult or not. (We qualify our conclusion with "may not" rather than "does not" because we have a colleague who works on Navajo, and the intricacies of that language make us wonder whether perhaps linguists are blithely leaving out Navajo when they arrive at such conclusions.) It might well be true, on the other hand, that it is harder for a speaker of a particular language X than for a speaker of a particular language Y to learn a particular language Z in adulthood. We carry the information we know about language from one language to the next as we learn new languages, and that may well affect the ease with which we learn the next language. Nevertheless, we don't know of any particular language K, for example, that stands out as being more difficult for speakers of all other languages to learn in adulthood.

When we respond to questions about language, sometimes our knowledge of particular languages and of the formal nature of linguistic principles helps us. This is particularly true if the questions are about how language is produced and processed or about particular sociolinguistic facts, such as differences between regional speech patterns. But we are struck by how often these questions could have been answered by anybody who took the time to seriously consider language use. Ordinary speakers have a great deal of knowledge about language, and if they apply common sense in analyzing language, they can debunk many common misconceptions.

Most people, however, have little idea of how to approach language questions. If you want to learn about language in a formal way, we encourage you to pick up a linguistics textbook or to take a linguistics course. However, if you want to learn how to look at language issues so that you can make sensible and responsible decisions about language in your daily life, then this book will help you.

Although there are two authors of this book, we divided up the work, with one of us taking the lead on each chapter. So the chapters use an *I* that is sometimes one of us and sometimes the other.

The chapters in this book are divided into two parts. Part I deals with language as a human ability. Part II deals with language in the context of society. At the end of each chapter is a list of readings for further consultation, as well as keywords for an Internet (e.g., Google) search. Another wonderful resource is the website of videos on language set up by the Linguistic Society of America: http://www.uga.edu/lsava/Archive.html.

The chapters invite you into one way of approaching language. They help you to uncover assumptions behind language questions so that you can evaluate them. They help you to recognize what sorts of things might be evidence for or against different positions on a language issue. And they help sort out the evidence in a systematic and methodologically sound way. Although only fifteen issues are addressed in this book, we hope that reading these chapters will give you the confidence to approach other language issues in a systematic way.

Linguistics is a field in which reasonable people can and do disagree. Nevertheless, in this book we are rarely equivocal (we are linguists, not politicians). However, the arguments are laid out step by step, so if you disagree at any point along the way, you can diverge and find your own answers, knowing, at least, what our position is and why.

Acknowledgments

Many people helped in writing the original edition of this book, and they are thanked there. Additionally, we thank all of our past and present students and colleagues, as well as Peter Ohlin, the linguistics editor for Oxford University Press and his team of Brian Hurley and Brian Desmond, who shepherded us through this revision.

Contents

Part I

Language: The Human Ability

1 How do we acquire language?

How did you and I learn to speak and understand language? This is a difficult question to approach because even though we've all done it, we can't remember doing it. Acquiring language begins in the womb for hearing fetuses, and our accessible memories don't go back that far.

Nevertheless, many of us might be willing to attempt an answer. After all, we acquired language, so we must know something about the process. But is this true? We metabolize sugar, but unless we've studied chemistry, we don't know how it's done. It happens naturally; the body does it on its own.

A common misconception is that children need to be taught language. In fact, though, acquiring language happens naturally—just like metabolizing sugar. No one has to teach us; our brain does it on its own. This chapter presents some of the important evidence.

Most of the time we can find evidence in our daily language experience that is relevant in evaluating hypotheses about how language works. One of the purposes of this book is to help you recognize that evidence. Therefore, I hesitate to draw on data that you don't have easy access to. However, sometimes relatively inaccessible data can be amazingly helpful, and this is one of those times. We begin by looking at data that you couldn't be expected to have access to if you hadn't studied linguistics. Our goal is to find out what factors are necessary and/or sufficient for language acquisition to take place.

Let's consider the idea that children need to be taught language in an explicit and conscious way. This is false. There are language communities in which no conscious language teaching goes on, but language acquisition proceeds normally. In Samoa, for example, adults do not view infants and small children as conversational partners, nor do they feel a responsibility to model their speech so that children can more easily learn it. Instead, the children simply overhear speech between adults. Likewise, the adults do not listen to the speech of the children. It's as though the children's talk is not part of the larger language community. Yet the children acquire the language of the larger community just fine and at the same rate that children acquire language all around the world. Conscious language teaching, then, is not necessary for first language acquisition.

A new possibility might come to you (as it often has to my students): Children in these communities must be learning solely by mimicking, so maybe mimicking is sufficient for language acquisition. That idea, however, is also wrong.

There have been instances in which children have grown to adolescence in (almost) complete linguistic deprivation. For example, there is a well-documented case of a child dubbed the Wild Boy of Aveyron. In 1799 a feral boy was found living in the woods of Aveyron in the south of France. His habits included eating off the floor and making noises that resembled canine sounds. All indications were that he had been raised by wild animals. Although Doctor Jean-Marc Itard, an educator who had much success in teaching speech to deaf children (the Wild Boy of Aveyron was not deaf), put years of work into trying to teach him human language, he never acquired more than a small vocabulary, with no sign of a system of rules for putting those words together into sentences.

Another example involves a girl researchers called Genie, who was discovered in 1970 in Los Angeles, living in captive isolation that limited both her physical activity and her linguistic input. At the time of her discovery, she could hardly walk and gave no indication of knowing what speech was. Several researchers worked for years to teach Genie language, but she never progressed beyond an unsystematic stringing together of a few words. In middle age, she stopped talking altogether, and her guardians removed her from the study.

There are other cases of children (often raised by depraved adults) who never acquired facility with language. Over and over again, adults (often researchers) taught these children to mimic, but mimicry did not result in language acquisition. Mimicry is not a sufficient means of acquiring language.

These are extreme cases. Most children, although not overtly corrected by their parents when they make linguistic mistakes, are exposed to a tremendous amount of language modeling. Also, most children do a lot of mimicry as part of the process of acquiring language. Nevertheless, overt teaching is not necessary, and mimicry is not sufficient. Instead, something else is the crucial factor, and it turns out to be biology.

For a couple of decades a team of researchers in London and Oxford studied members of a British family who exhibited an inherited and rare language disorder. Finally, they found another child, not related, who exhibited the same severe disorder. This led to the discovery in 2001 of a gene, called FOXP2, that is directly involved in language ability. There is no doubt: Language is a biological matter, and humans diverged from chimps and other primate lineages in this regard approximately 4.6 to 6.2 million years ago.

For the past half century, linguists have hypothesized that there is a language mechanism in the brain, an actual physical mechanism that is responsible for all aspects of language, including learning, processing, and production. This mechanism is probably physiologically discontinuous. That is, it is not a single whole, like a kidney, liver, or other major organ. Instead, various parts of the language mechanism are located in separate spots in the brain, and they work together to produce comprehensive language ability. The failure of the Wild Boy of Aveyron and of Genie to acquire language is taken as evidence that the language mechanism somehow changes at an early age, perhaps the age of five (although we don't know for sure since we cannot ethically do experiments), so the ability to acquire a first language after that critical period is diminished or even erased.

Further evidence for the existence of the language mechanism comes from data on linguistic damage and language pathologies. It's commonly known that strokes can result in severe language loss in a person whose intelligence is otherwise left intact. There are also several other types of damage to the brain that cause particular language impairments, and, significantly, if the site of the damage is known, the symptoms are predictable. For example, damage to the front part of the brain's left hemisphere results in the loss of the ability to use a coherent word order and general sentence structure. The afflicted person produces short and choppy utterances and exhibits a general lack of fluency. This condition is known as Broca's aphasia. Damage to the rear part of the brain's left hemisphere results in the loss of the ability to use words appropriate to meaning, to interpret language, or both. It is known as Wernicke's aphasia. Damage to the brain's entire left hemisphere results in all of these malfunctions and is known as global aphasia.

In such instances, damage has been done to different parts of the language mechanism.

Also, certain pathologies are linked to congenital problems. For example, children born with spina bifida sometimes experience devastating retardation. Nevertheless, they can articulately recount imagined events (events that never occurred), sounding entirely of normal intelligence when they do so. Here the language mechanism clearly operates independently of the damaged intelligence. Some children are born with a set of syndromes that have been called specific language impairment (SLI). These children do not have abnormal intelligence or any kind of sensory or emotional, social, or behavioral problems. Their problems have specifically to do with language issues; they have trouble understanding language and producing well-formed sentences. Again, the language mechanism has a pathology independent of any other brain function.

Once we've concluded that a language mechanism exists in the brain as a physical entity and that it changes over time, the question of how we acquire a first language is similar to that of how we metabolize sugar in that any biological function has to be studied scientifically to be understood.

I'm now going to present data I have collected on first language acquisition. Some are rather ordinary, but others I sought out to make my point. Although the data are largely anecdotal, in every instance there are studies, based on large data corpuses, that show that these cases are representative of ordinary language acquisition (unless I explicitly say otherwise).

Let's start with newborns. Here's the first scene: A baby fresh from the hospital is in his grandmother's arms, crying continuously. The grandmother, who has flown in from Florida for the occasion, is singing and cooing and cuddling the newborn to her breast. The mother comes through the door and coos as she crosses the room. At the first sound of her voice, the baby's cries turn to gulps that cease by the time the mother reaches him. What is the baby responding to? When the mother first came through the door, she was too far away for him to smell her, and the grandmother is holding him in such a way that his eyes can take in only his grandmother's face and chest. It appears that this newborn recognizes his mother's voice.

At the beginning of this chapter, I claimed that language acquisition starts in the womb. Around the seventh month of gestation, the auditory system is formed and, except in an instance of a hard-of-hearing or deaf fetus, functions well enough to be able to listen to the world outside the womb. It's not surprising, then, that (hearing) newborns come into the world recognizing the voices of their mother and of those people who constantly surround their mother. Surely the newborns are not consciously trying to acquire language. They simply listen to the world, yet already they have learned to pick out certain sounds as relevant to their various needs and wants.

Here's a second scene: I gave a talk to a social club of Korean women living in Ann Arbor, Michigan, all of whom sent their children to Korean school on Saturday to keep the language alive among their offspring. After the talk, my husband came in with our four-month-old son, Robert. I put Robert in the arms of one of the Korean women and went to the refreshments area for sandwiches. The women exclaimed over him in Korean. There was a constant coming and going of women who were peeking into his face and touching his hair and back. He gazed around happily, his eyes going from the women to the furniture to the lights (he loved lights). Then I whispered to a food server to please go over and say something, pretty much anything, to Robert. She did. And when he heard her speak, he turned to her immediately and gave her a giant smile and started to babble. She spoke English, her native language, which is the language Robert was used to hearing at home.

To conclude that Robert could distinguish English from Korean might seem rash, given this one instance. Nonetheless, studies on children even younger than Robert show that English-speaking children can pick out English from French and other languages, just as French-speaking children can pick out French from English and other languages. In these studies the children's recognition of English is indicated by increased eye activity and heartbeat rather than the smile and babbling that Robert produced, but the studies were done under laboratory conditions, whereas Robert's situation was a social one. So by very early in the first year of life, children have somehow managed to separate, from all of the various noises they encounter, not just speech sounds but also the speech sounds of their own, native language. They are on the road to acquiring the sound system of their language.

Here's a third scene: A mother carries her ten-month-old into the child's bedroom. She says, "Want to turn on the light, Maggie? Go on. Press." Maggie's mouth opens, and she twists in her mother's arms and presses the wall switch. The overhead light goes on. "La," says Maggie. "That's right," says her mother, "you turned on the light. You're such a smart girl."

Maggie picked out the word *light* from the stream of her mother's talk. If you look at that stream, it's rather complicated. This mother did not use any of the special devices that some people use when talking with babies—so called motherese. She didn't say, for example, "Baby turn on light? Light light. See the light?" where the very preponderance of the word *light* could have been a clue. Instead, the mother talked to her baby daughter in ordinary language. Nevertheless, Maggie processed the speech well enough to know what to do. In fact, studies have shown that children exposed to ordinary talk acquire speech at the same rate as those exposed to large amounts of motherese.

You may object to my analysis, saying that this scene doesn't show that Maggie picked out the word *light* since turning on the light is probably part of the nighttime routine. Maggie is primed not just by the word *light* but also by all the other factors that mark this routine (she's just had her bath, and they're going into the bedroom). Maybe if the mother hadn't said anything, Maggie would still have reached around and turned on the light.

So I encourage you to test that hypothesis. Find a child like Maggie who likes to turn on lights. Then hold the child and stand near a wall switch but with your back to it so that you aren't making the task obvious. Ask the child to turn on the light. I can't guess what the child will do, but the point is that you can test your hypothesis. If you're going to take a scientific approach to the question of how we learn language, you need to come up with testable hypotheses and actually test them.

What is undeniable is that children do learn to pick out individual words. The literature on first language acquisition points to the first birthday as the time when most children start to produce words. Then at some point during their second year, they move into a two-word phase, in which one word refers to an object, and the other operates on the object in some way. Typical utterances are these:

> More grape.
> All gone.
> Daddy shoe.
> Doggy good.

Sometime around the child's third birthday, give or take six months, language takes a giant leap, and children start producing long sentences with varying degrees of morphological and syntactic complexity. Typical utterances at this stage are these:

What that girl doing? She get hurt.
I wrote this. See?
Time to go. Put your shoes on. We got to hurry.
Let me do it, me, don't help.
You can't talk. No. Don't talk.
Eva cry. Somebody hurt Eva.

Some utterances can be much more complex. My oldest daughter was two years and seven months old when her brother was born. Two weeks after his birth, she climbed into the center of my husband's and my bed and said:

Nobody doesn't love me no more.

When my oldest son was two years and four months, he came running in from the backyard and said:

Oh, Mamma, somebody made cacca in my pants.

By this point (two years old) children can produce thousands of words, and by the time they are four years old they will have acquired all of the elements of language, though their mastery of details can take many more years.

All of the generalizations I have reported to you about the one-word phase, the two-word phase, and eventual sentences come from the literature on first language acquisition. In my own family experience, with five children, some of the generalizations I reported do not hold. Both my husband and I always spoke to our children in ordinary language. We spoke to them a lot and also read and sang to them. Two of our children started producing single words around the age of nine months, one started at six months, and another said almost nothing until she was two. Then one day as we were reading a book together, she pointed at a butterfly and said, "Bubbafwy." I was so excited that I called the family together and asked Eva to say it again, but she smiled at me and remained silent. She really didn't say much else until she turned three, at which point she went from single-word utterances to two-word utterances to constant (and I mean incessant) chattering in the span of about a month. My middle child acquired language in a way that confounded me entirely. I'd say, "What would you like to drink, Nick?" And he'd answer, "Awamih," with an intonation drop on the last syllable. Then he'd reach for the milk. One day when he was one year and five months old, I decided to try to help him learn in an explicit way. So I said, "Nick, you have to say 'milk' if you want milk." Nick looked at me earnestly and said vehemently, "Awamih." I said slowly and loudly, "Milk. You have to say 'milk.'" Nick said slowly and loudly, "Awamih." That's when I finally got it. He was saying, "I want milk," a whole sentence, not just a single word. His intonation should have told me that all along. Nick never went through the one-word or two-word phase. He simply spoke in sentences, sentences that were extremely hard for me to catch since his mastery of the sound system of English was typical for his age. Until he was around two, most people outside the family didn't know what he was saying, but we, at least, finally understood.

My point here is not to say that the researchers are wrong but that acquiring language, like learning to walk, run, or skip, occurs in different ways with different children. There may be a canonical pattern that we can all point to, but the fact remains that we (as individuals) might not know a single given child who actually went through the exact stages reported in the literature during the exact time periods predicted despite the fact that the statistics can be verified in repeated experiments.

When first language acquisition involves exposure to two (or more) languages rather than one, we talk about a bi- or multi-lingual upbringing. The following are some data and experiences giving you an insight into the linguistically interesting aspects of this kind of upbringing.

Although my coauthor and her husband are raising their son Niko in the United States, where he is surrounded by English, she speaks her native language, German, with Niko. Since he is a two-year-old who does not yet go to preschool, he is exposed to English and German pretty much evenly. Her husband speaks English with Niko, and Niko hears his parents speak English to each other, but when Niko is spending time with his mother exclusively, he communicates with her mainly in German. When they're on the playground, and the caretakers of other children find out that Niko and his mother speak German to each other, their reaction is almost always something like, "Oh, wow, you're teaching him German!" While my coauthor shares their enthusiasm about bringing up her child bilingually and is glad that other people are interested, she always feels the need to explain that she's not actually teaching him anything. Just as the acquisition of one native language is an unconscious process that happens automatically as long as the child gets enough exposure to that language, the acquisition of an additional language is not something a parent can teach the child. It's more a matter of commitment and discipline to consistently speak the additional language than of being a good teacher.

Whether a family exposes a young child to one, two, or even more languages, the attempt to correct the child by saying something like "No, don't say X, say Y" won't work. At the moment (at the age of twenty-five months), when my coauthor's son Niko talks about one of his favorite activities in English, he tends to say, "Niko is drewing." His mother's response is "Yes, you are drawing. Du malst [the equivalent in German]." Although Niko might repeat the correct English version of the sentence after her, the next time the same situation comes up, perhaps later in the day or the next day, the chances are that he will say something like "I will drew a little." So, it's obvious that the base form of the verb *draw* is stored in Niko's mental lexicon as *drew*, and this won't change until Niko's language mechanism has gotten sufficient evidence to make the switch from *drew* to *draw*. A few instances of modeling *draw* instead of *drew* in situations like this one apparently aren't sufficient. Of course, Niko hears *drew* a lot, too. Whenever his parents talk about his favorite activity as something that has happened in the past, they say "drew," so it is not surprising that it will take some time for Niko to sort out these verb forms, storing *draw* as the present (base) form and *drew* as the past form.

A commonly held belief about bringing children up bilingually is that it will confuse the child unnecessarily and slow down the language acquisition process. While some bilingual children have indeed been reported to take slightly longer with native language fluency than the average monolingual child, this delay does not have any negative consequences in the long run. If anything, bilingual children have advantages over monolingual children. They have better mental flexibility and cognitive control that persists through late adulthood and may delay the onset of dementia by as much as four years. Additionally, they have the benefit of feeling at home in more than one culture. Keep in mind also that many bilingual children are not at all delayed in their language acquisition process. Niko spoke in both English and German relatively early. Now, at the age of twenty-five months, he is already attempting to express himself in complete sentences and often succeeds. A few hours before the time of this writing, for example, he and his mother were driving in the car together, talking about what kinds of construction site vehicles they were seeing on the side of the road. She pointed out in German that she didn't see the steamroller that they usually see there, and a moment later he said, putting the six words in exactly the right order with exactly the right grammatical inflections (endings), "Ich habe doch die Walze gesehen" ('I did see the steamroller'). The point is, regardless of whether they are being raised monolingually or bilingually, some children start speaking earlier than others. As explained earlier, there's a huge range.

So how is it all happening, whether in one language or more? Consider the utterance "More grape." This was said as a request at lunch. Notice that the child didn't say "Grape more." Word order is well in place in this child's utterance, as in all the earlier two-word utterances. Go out and listen to children. They rarely scramble words, although they are exposed to many words in various orders in different sentences. The child may even have been exposed to these exact words in the opposite order. Consider these sentences:

> I like **grape more** than orange.
> He's **gone all** the time.
> This is the **shoe Daddy** fixed.
> What a **good doggy**.

The boldfaced words are in reverse order from the children's two-word utterances given earlier. So the word order the children use cannot be due simply to exposure. Somehow children are fitting words into the proper order for the meaning that they want—proper with respect to their native language. A child who speaks a language that has operators that follow the objects they operate on (such as German, a language in which the verb follows the object in dependent clauses, giving something like *Buch lesen* ('book read') instead of "read book"), for example, will use word order opposite from that of a child who speaks English, at least in certain contexts. That is, children arrange their words according to abstract linguistic principles that no one explicitly teaches them.

Likewise, whereas children's early utterances are often brief, they have structure. Thus, corresponding to the adult utterance

When are you coming?

the child might say:

When?

or:

When come?

but would never say:

Are?

or:

When you?

The child's utterance is not simply a truncation of the adult's. It has a grammar, and that grammar gradually develops into the mature grammar.

In fact, many children are exposed to ungrammatical language, yet they produce grammatical language. Consider, for example, a situation that many of us have witnessed: children of immigrants who have at best only a rudimentary knowledge of English. These children hear their parents saying sentences such as "Paper no come today," but the children produce, "The paper didn't come today." Instead of mimicking their parents (who might even be making a word-for-word translation from their native language into English), these children use the language they hear in the world outside the family. They glean the linguistic rules of English from sentences spoken by native speakers, who have a coherent grammar, not from the sentences spoken by their parents, who might well have an incoherent grammar in English.

Even more striking facts hold in a situation that most of us have probably not witnessed: children of parents who speak a pidgin—a language put together piecemeal by adults of varying languages who are thrown together and must communicate however they can. These children hear utterances that do not conform to recognizable principles of natural language grammar, yet they produce speech that does conform to such principles: They speak a creole language. (Both pidgins and creoles are discussed in chapter 9.) Once more, it's clear that children are using principles that must be encoded somehow in the language mechanism—principles of natural language that are fundamental and thus form what linguists call universal grammar, or UG.

Finally, consider the case of cryptophasia (secret languages), often used at home. Many children, when left with other children for long periods, will develop special ways of talking together. This is quite common, although for most children the game of creating a language loses its attraction fairly quickly, so the secret language is abandoned before it might become fully formed. Sometimes, however, the language blossoms. There are studies of such languages between twins, called *twin language*, and other studies have focused on sign languages within a family, called *home sign*. Significantly, twin languages and home sign exhibit natural grammars; they conform to UG. In the former cases, the twins also speak a community language, so one might argue that the UG characteristics of twin language are carried over from the community language. However, in some of the instances of home sign, the child signers, at least, do not participate in any other community language but do not introduce nonnatural elements into their signs. Thus, language created by children conforms to UG even when the children have no access to any community language.

We are hard-wired to process and produce natural human language. We acquire our specific native language in a natural way by sifting through what we are exposed to or what we create with the UG principles that we are born with. The data presented here from other cultures and those on linguistically deprived children and on the biology of language all make this point. Importantly, however, we could arrive at this conclusion on our own, without these rather esoteric data, by looking scientifically at examples of children's language. Methodical study of relevant language data can take us a long way.

Further Readings

Berwick, R. 1985. *The acquisition of syntactic knowledge*. Cambridge, Mass.: MIT Press.

Bialystok, E., F. Craik, and M. Freedman. 2007. Bilingualism as a protection against the onset of symptoms of dementia. *Neuropsychologia* 45(2): 459–64.

Bialystok, E., F. Craik, R. Klein, and M. Viswanathan. 2004. Bilingualism, aging, and cognitive control: Evidence from the Simon task. *Psychology and Aging* 19: 290–303.

Bosch, L., and N. Sebastian-Galles. 2001. Evidence of early language discrimination abilities in infants from bilingual environments. *Infancy* 2(1): 29–49.

Brown, R. 1973. *A first language: The early stages*. Cambridge, Mass.: Harvard University Press.

Chomsky, N. 1975. *Reflections on language*. New York: Random House.

Clark, E. 1993. *The lexicon in acquisition*. New York: Cambridge University Press.

Guasti, M. T. 2002. *Language acquisition: The growth of grammar*. Cambridge, Mass.: MIT Press.

Heath, S. 1983. *Ways with words: Language, life, and work in communities and classrooms*. New York: Cambridge University Press.

Ingram, D. 1989. *First language acquisition: Method, description, and explanation*. New York: Cambridge University Press.

Lai, C., S. Fisher, J. Hurst, F. Vargha-Khadems, and A. Monaco. 2001. A forkhead-domain gene is mutated in severe speech and language disorder. *Nature* 413: 519–23.

Language acquisition. http://www.facstaff.bucknell.edu/rbeard/acquisition.html (accessed May 3, 2009).

Locke, J. 1993. *The child's path to spoken language*. Cambridge, Mass.: Harvard University Press.

Pinker, S. 1984. *Language learnability and language development*. Cambridge, Mass.: Harvard University Press.

———. 1994. *The language instinct*. New York: Morrow.

———. Language acquisition. http://www.cogsci.soton.ac.uk/~harnad/Papers/Py104/pinker.langacq.html (accessed May 3, 2009).

Saffran, J., A. Senghas, and J. Trueswell. 2001. The acquisition of language by children. http://www.pnas.org/content/98/23/12874.full (accessed May 3, 2009).

Slobin, D., ed. 1985–1992. *The crosslinguistic study of language acquisition*. 3 vols. Hillsdale, N.J.: Erlbaum.

Tufts University child and family web guide. Language development. http://www.cfw.tufts.edu/topic/4/78.htm (accessed May 3, 2009).

Wexler, K., and P. Culicover. 1980. *Formal principles of language acquisition*. Cambridge, Mass.: MIT Press.

Keywords

first language acquisition
bilingual language acquisition
innateness of language

2 What is linguistics?

In the preface of this book, my coauthor and I introduce ourselves as linguists who are teaching linguistics. We also refer you to a linguistics textbook if you want to be introduced to the formal study of linguistics. But what does all this mean? What is the formal study of linguistics, and what do linguists do exactly?

Going for walks with my two-year-old son and taking him to the local playgrounds, I meet a lot of nice people who ask what my job is. When I say that I teach at Swarthmore College, their faces light up, and the next question is, "What do you teach?" As they hear my answer, people usually react in one of two ways. Some immediately follow up with, "Oh, great. How many languages do you speak?" Others look confused. The polite, though slightly hesitant, smile on their faces tells me that they are lost, trying very hard to process and categorize the information but don't know what to make of my answer. If they are brave enough, they ask me to clarify: "So, what kinds of classes do you teach then?" Good question.

As a linguist, you don't necessarily speak very many languages. In fact, linguists like to distinguish between polyglots and linguists—intersecting but distinct sets. Though some linguists get into the field because they have a knack for effortlessly learning exotic languages, this is not the norm. There's also a significant difference between linguists and philologists. The latter, literally people who love words, articulation, and reason, are primarily concerned with rhetoric, interpretation of literature, and historical linguistics (etymology and language change), most commonly through the examination of texts, rather than spoken language. Linguists, on the other hand, work most commonly with a spoken language corpus, and, while literary studies may be of interest to them, they are not generally the focus of examination.

Getting back to the issue of how many languages linguists speak, we note that linguistics students typically start with the knowledge of their native language as a base and learn how to break down and analyze it. They investigate this language in terms of its sound system (if it is a spoken language—if it's a sign language, in terms of its manual articulatory system) and patterns (phonetics and phonology, respectively), its word and sentence structure (morphology and syntax, respectively), and its system of deriving sentence and discourse meaning (semantics and pragmatics, respectively). The goal is to develop a model of the language mechanism humans are born with, more precisely, what the principles of universal grammar (UG) are (see chapter 1). Starting with one language, the native language of the majority of the students in the class, we come up with a set of rules that produces the attested or grammatical utterances of the language and does not allow the production of unattested or ungrammatical ones.

When I talk about grammatical utterances, you may think of sentences that adhere to rules like the following:

> Don't end a sentence with a preposition!
> Don't split infinitives!
> Don't say "me" in subject or predicate nominative position, say "I"!

However, these are not the kinds of rules linguists are interested in. These are rules children are taught in school when they learn to speak and write "proper" English (see chapter 8). So-called proper English is a certain style of English appropriate for formal situations like job interviews or essay writing, but it is not what linguists are referring to when they talk about grammatical utterances. More precisely, breaking the rules of "proper" English does not necessarily lead to ungrammaticality. Utterances like the following are perfectly grammatical despite violating the preceding rules:

> That's the boy I'm going to the movies with.
> It's better to carefully avoid splitting infinitives.
> Who is it?—It's me.

Pretty much anything native speakers of a language may say or hear and perceive as a naturally occurring utterance, that is, not a mistake that perhaps a nonnative speaker would make, is considered grammatical by linguists. Notice that it's what native speakers say that linguists are interested in, not so much what they write. In writing, especially formal letter writing, paper writing, and news report writing, we tend to stick to the rules of the "proper" English we learned in school. There are many more things we would say or hear and find acceptable than there are things that we would write and judge acceptable if specifically asked. So, if linguists want to gain insight into the mental (subconscious) grammar that people have in their heads, they are better off focusing on spoken than on written language.

Here are some examples of truly ungrammatical utterances—ungrammatical in the linguistic sense. Can you identify the source of ungrammaticality in each example?

> *That's the boy I'm going to movies with.
> *It's better to carefully avoid to split infinitives.
> *Who it is?—It's me.

(The asterisk indicates an ungrammatical utterance.)

In the first example, there's a missing determiner (article). We say "going to the movies" (not "going to movies") when we are talking about wanting to go to a movie theater (as opposed to just going to see movies, whether in the theater or not, as in "I like going to movies"). In the second example, *avoid* is followed by *to* plus the nonfinite form of the verb rather than a verb in the *-ing* form. Finally, in the third example, the word order in the *who*-question is wrong: *It* and *is* should be reversed. In grammatical direct questions, the first verb (here *is*) immediately follows the question word (here *who*). Only in embedded questions like "I don't know who it is" does the subject (here *it*) immediately follow the question word. These are the kinds of language rules linguists are interested in, rules that you follow automatically and probably are not consciously aware of, rules that simply describe the way native speakers talk. The rules of "proper" English discussed earlier, which typically start with *don't*, are prescriptive in that they are intended to keep speakers from saying things they would naturally say. The rules linguists come up with in order to derive the grammatical utterances of a language, then, are descriptive in nature, describing how people actually speak, not prescriptive, telling them what not to say.

Once we have a working hypothesis for the set of rules that governs our native language, we compare them to the rules of other languages in order to make our set as general as possible. After all, we are born with the bare bones of a set of universal principles. At this point in the classroom discussion, students bring in their knowledge of other languages they may have been exposed to beyond the one examined in the classroom, or they may even investigate a new language to offer comparisons. Every linguist who knows the International Phonetic Alphabet (IPA) has access to transcribed utterances of any language and can therefore investigate these utterances in the way described here. However, linguists who want to discover facts about the rule system of a language that has not yet been recorded in the literature are better off being somewhat fluent speakers of the language, so that they can spend time with native speakers and elicit data (i.e., record their speech). This is why many linguists do speak more than one language. A better question than "How many languages do you speak?" then probably is "What language(s) do you specialize in?"

To get back to the very reasonable question of what kinds of classes linguistics professors teach, the subdisciplines of theoretical linguistics are divided into the core areas of investigation mentioned earlier: phonetics, phonology, morphology, syntax, semantics, pragmatics. And that's what the corresponding classes are titled as well.

For example, the human body can make a range of sounds, but only a small subset of those made by the vocal tract (the mouth, nose, pharynx, larynx) are used in language. Moreover, different languages have different (although highly overlapping) inventories of sounds. The study of how we produce language sounds is called *articulatory phonetics*. The study of the physical properties of those sounds is called *acoustic phonetics*.

Individual sounds don't typically occur in isolation in speech but rather in the company of other sounds, and they change their shape accordingly. So in American English the word *hot* has a "t" sound, written in IPA as [t], at the end of it. However, when we (Americans, that is—Brits say it differently) say the phrase *hot air*, there is no [t] (what you hear instead is called a *flap*). The study of the rules involved in such sound changes is called *phonology*. Notice that sounds can change not just in their quality (that is, a [t] versus a [d], for example) but also in their quantity. Thus, some languages distinguish between short and long consonants and/ or vowels. Issues of duration are part of the study of phonology. Additionally, you can take a vowel such as [a] ("ah") and sing it in a low pitch, a high pitch, or alternating pitches. Also, in some languages, pitch (as in modern Greek) or tone (as in Chinese) can be the distinguishing factor between two different words, just as stress can in other languages (say the following words in two different ways, and you'll get a sense of what I mean: *convert, record, consort*). All of these factors are part of the study of phonology.

Additionally, words are made up not just of sound units but also of meaning units. The word *unkindly*, for example, has three meaningful parts: *un-*, *kind*, and *-ly*, and those parts must occur in precisely that order. We don't say *lyunkind* or *kindlyun* or any of the other permutations possible of those three units. The study of the rules that govern how we put the meaningful parts of words together is called *morphology*. Languages have a range of ways they can build words. With *unkindly* we see concatenation: A prefix and a suffix have simply been slapped onto the root *kind*. However, there are lots of other ways to build words. Languages can make changes in the sounds of words with resulting effects on meaning, so that you find pairings comparable, for example, to English *blood/bleed*, where a difference in the vowels correlates with the difference between a noun and a verb. In English, such pairs are relatively isolated, but in some languages sound change of that sort is productive (that is, highly predictable). All the different ways languages manipulate meaning within words fall under the rubric of morphology.

Just as sounds don't typically occur in isolation, words also usually occur in the context of other words. They go together to form phrases and sentences. Nonetheless, we don't just throw words together randomly. Instead, in English statements, we generally put the verb between the subject and the object, while in Japanese (and in German dependent clauses), we put the verb at the end, after the subject and the object, and in Irish we put the verb first, before the subject and the object. The study of how we organize words into phrases and sentences is called syntax. If you noticed that in our descriptions of English, Japanese (German), and Irish, the subject always preceded the object and the only variable was where the verb was located, you noticed the sort of thing that linguists look for when they are seeking to discover the principles that govern the rules of syntax in any given language. While it is not entirely unproblematic, there is a strong tendency for languages to place subjects before objects (or, some might argue, the more agentive-like participant in an event before the more patient-like participant in that event). All of these sorts of issues make up the study of syntax.

In English, depending on how the words in a sentence are put together, they add up to a different sentence meaning. The study of linguistic meaning is called semantics. In "Mary loves John," for example, Mary is the agent involved in the event of loving, and John is the *theme* or *patient* of the event. If *John* precedes the verb and *Mary* follows it, as in "John loves Mary," then their roles in the event are reversed. We say that the verb *love* expresses a predicate (here, an act) with two arguments, the agent and the theme/patient. Other verbs, like *sleep* and *fall*, have only one argument. In the case of *sleep*, this one argument fulfills the agent role, whereas in the case of *fall*, it fulfills the theme/patient role. Also, depending on whether we use nouns with a definite, an indefinite, or no determiner (e.g., *the, a, these*), the denotation (meaning) of the noun phrase headed by that noun changes. (A noun with all of its paraphernalia (which, might, in fact, be nothing at all) is a noun phrase, and the noun heads the phrase. So *dog* is the head of the noun phrase *that crazy dog I just bought*. However, *dogs* is both the head of the phrase and the whole phrase in *I like dogs*.) Generally (although you can easily come up with special cases that don't fit this pattern and need further analysis), a definite determiner like *the* or *these* denotes specific entities, and an indefinite determiner like *a* or no determiner at all denotes generic, unspecified entities. In order to represent sentence meaning, both complex and simple, semanticists use formal languages borrowed from the field of philosophy, for example, propositional logic and predicate logic. All of the intricacies that contribute to the exact meaning of a sentence and the task of representing this meaning formally are dealt with in the study of semantics.

Pragmatics is generally considered a subfield of semantics, and it is primarily concerned not with the denotations of individual words and how they combine to derive sentence meaning but with how the context in which a sentence is uttered influences its meaning. The utterance "I'd love a glass of water," for example, takes on very different shades of meaning depending on where and when it is uttered. In a restaurant, this utterance will probably be interpreted as a request directed toward the waiter, and one expects that the waiter will bring a glass of water to the table. Somewhere out in a desert, however, the same utterance is more likely to be interpreted as an unfulfillable wish. Thus, although the literal meaning of two utterances (what is often called the truth-functional meaning, that is, the conditions under which a sentence is true), computed compositionally by adding up the meaning of the words in the sentence, could be exactly the same, their communicative meaning could be very different. Pragmatics also takes into consideration people's life experiences and knowledge of how the world works. Depending on the common ground (that is, the mutual understanding of the language situation) that speaker and listener share, utterances come with certain implications. These are messages that, though not literally pronounced, are nonetheless part of what utterances communicate (you will encounter these types of hidden messages again in chapter 13, where we discuss issues of language and power).

If you see a car stopped on the side of the road, for example, and you have the following exchange with the driver of the car, you both know you've said enough to get your respective points across:

Speaker A: Hi. I ran out of gas.
Speaker B: There's a Shell just down the road.

Speaker A's utterance implies that he needs help. So, he is really asking something like, "Could you tell me what to do?" Speaker B's utterance implies that there is a place nearby where Speaker A can get gas. Assuming that *Shell*, the name of a gas station, is part of the common ground, no further explanation is needed. Context-dependent derivation of meaning like this is the core of the study of pragmatics.

These are the core areas of linguistics—what is called theoretical linguistics. Why should we study theoretical linguistics? People have been interested in the workings of the human brain for millennia. Language offers a window into the brain that for many years was more transparent than other windows since the data were so apparent: All you had to do was study what people said. Now that we have brain scans, we have other quite transparent windows into the brain. We can see what parts of the brain are active when certain events take place (visual events, language events, motor events, and so on). Still, even with brain scans, we are a long way from being able to determine precisely what happens in the brain when we use a contraction (such as "I'm" instead of "I am"), for example. So the study of linguistics allows us to come up with the set of subconscious rules that operates in any given language. In addition, the comparison of these rules across languages allows us to formulate the set of subconscious principles that governs these rules. And the principles tell us something about the way the human mind organizes information. Basically, then, linguistics is a branch of cognitive science.

Additional classes offered by linguistics programs, besides those covering the core areas, focus on the overlap of theoretical linguistics with other disciplines. Since language is involved in almost every human interaction, the study of language is relevant to a multitude of disciplines such as psychology, sociology, computer science, philosophy, and anthropology. These classes of applied linguistics are typically called psycholinguistics (which includes the study of language acquisition; see chapter 1), sociolinguistics (which includes the study of language variation and endangerment; see all of part II but in particular chapters 8, 9, 10, and 15), computational linguistics (see chapter 7), and language and philosophy (logic). Another important subdiscipline and type of linguistics class not mentioned yet is historical linguistics, which deals mainly with how languages change over time (see chapters 8 and 11).

So, that's what linguistics is and what linguists do, at least generally speaking. As stated in the preface, many questions addressed in this book can be answered just by tapping into your knowledge of language, using common sense, certainly if guided by the informal discussions provided in the chapters of this book. However, the question of "What is linguistics?" needs a specific answer that I simply wanted to spell out for you.

Further Readings

Bach, Emmon. 1989. *Informal lectures on formal semantics*. Albany: SUNY Press.

Bergmann, A., K. Currie Hall, and S. M. Ross, eds. 2007. *Language files: Materials for an introduction to language and linguistics*, 10th ed. Columbus: Ohio State University Press.

Campbell, L. 2004. *Historical linguistics: An introduction*, 2nd ed. Cambridge, Mass.: MIT Press.

Carnie, A. 2006. *Syntax: A generative introduction*, 2nd ed. Oxford: Wiley-Blackwell.

Chomsky, N. 2006. http://www.chomsky.info/ (accessed May 3, 2009).

Field, J. 2003. *Psycholinguistics: A resource book for students*. London: Routledge.

Fromkin, V., R. Rodman, and N. Hyams. 2007. *An introduction to language*, 8th ed. Boston: Thomson Wadsworth.

Hurford, J., M. Studdert-Kennedy, and C. Knight, eds. 1998. *Approaches to the evolution of language: Social and cognitive bases*. New York: Cambridge University Press.

Jurafsky, D., and J. Martin. 2008. *Speech and language processing: An introduction to natural language processing, computational linguistics, and speech recognition*, 2nd ed. Upper Saddle River, N.J.: Prentice-Hall.

Morris, M. 2006. *An introduction to the philosophy of language*. New York: Cambridge University Press.

Wardhaugh, R. 2006. *An introduction to sociolinguistics*. London: Blackwell.

Keywords

linguistics
morphology
phonetics
phonology
pragmatics
semantics
syntacs

3 From one language to the next: Why is it hard to learn a second language? Why is translation so difficult?

In the first chapter we looked at first language acquisition. There are important differences between acquiring a first language—a process that happens naturally to any child who is not linguistically deprived—and learning a second. The use of the word *acquiring* in one case and *learning* in the other is not accidental. Scholars debate, in fact, whether or not the cognitive faculties that are employed in second language learning are distinct from those employed in first language acquisition, and much of the evidence suggests that they are.

First, anyone who is learning a second language has already acquired a first language, so the language mechanism in the brain has already had certain linguistic parameters (such as word order) set, making the task quite different. What one needs to learn are the specific rules of the second language—often called the target language. The first language typically serves as the model, and errors often result from taking words from the target language and stringing them together by applying rules from the first language. So, for example, if the first language is English, and the target language is Japanese, a second language learner might position the Japanese verb between the subject and the object of the sentence, using the English word order, rather than placing the verb after the object, which is the correct Japanese word order. The greater the difference between the first language and the target language, the more tasks are involved in learning the latter. Second language learning can even be characterized as a gradual shift from the first language orientation to the target language orientation.

Second, first language acquisition takes place in early childhood (by the age of five usually) and typically cannot take place after that critical period. However, second language learning, especially in a classroom setting, proceeds more quickly with adults and adolescents than with younger children initially, although ultimately the younger child will become more proficient in the second language than the adolescent or adult. That is, second language learning proceeds more quickly with people who have a high proficiency in their first language.

Third, whereas first language acquisition happens without conscious teaching, second language learning generally does not. Thus, the process is distinct. Studies have shown that self-confidence, motivation, good self-image, and low anxiety are traits that improve facility in a second language, but none of these traits is important to first language acquisition.

Fourth, the complexity of the input affects second language learning but not first language acquisition. For example, if a second language learner has a classroom teacher who talks in the target language at a quick rate, in complex sentences, and about complicated matters, the learner will have a harder time initially than if simpler constructions are presented about matters that don't involve a lot of decision making or mental judgment. However, first language acquisition proceeds at the same rate whether or not adults simplify their language.

Fifth, practice is important for second language learning but not so much for first language acquisition. Even very quiet children acquire their first language at the ordinary rate.

The two processes have some things in common, however. Second language learning proceeds more quickly if the target language is used as the medium of instruction. So exposure to ordinary language is important, just as it is in first language acquisition, although it can help if that language is a little bit slower and less complex initially. In fact, second language learning is more successful when richly interactive language is used in the classroom. Instructional conversations are better teaching tools than memorization drills or lectures and recitations. And certainly conversations are more like the ordinary language one is exposed to in first language acquisition than are memorization drills and the like.

So far I've presented several generalizations that you can find in the literature on second language learning, and I haven't introduced any controversy. In chapter 12 we put ourselves in one situation that some second language learners face. However, that chapter is mainly about language policy, and it doesn't deal extensively with the kinds of questions posed to people who are learning a second language. Here, I want to look at precisely those types of questions. I do so by turning to the issue of translation, which allows us rather quickly to wrestle with a wide range of issues relevant to second language learning.

One Italian saying is "traduttori, traditori," literally, 'translators, traitors.' The idea is that translation can never be perfect, so anyone who translates necessarily betrays the original.

Various types of activities fall under the rubric of translation. The Certificate of Foreign Status of Beneficial Owner for United States Tax Withholding form (federal tax document form W-8BEN) asks in part 1, line 1, for "Name of individual or organization that is the beneficial owner." When a recent Norwegian visitor to my college read this phrase aloud and asked what it meant, the administrative assistant said, "Let me translate: 'you.'" Here the word *translate* was used to refer to an explanation through rewording within a language (intralingual translation).

Another way in which the word *translation* is used can be seen in the following situation. One of my college students wrote a poem, and another one did a dance that she called a translation of the poem. Here the word refers to an interpretation of one medium in another (intersemiotic translation).

I want to restrict the discussion to a third sense of *translation*, the commonest and the one most relevant to second language learning—interpreting from one human language into another human language, the activity the Italian saying claims is impossible to do with total accuracy (interlingual translation). Is the saying right? Or is true translation possible?

Students in high school language classes are continually asked to translate between languages. Probably you've been asked to do that, and you might even be able to remember some of the questions you faced. However, rather than make a list of the types of potential issues that come up, let's just jump into a translation exercise together.

We could choose a variety of texts to translate, for some of which the only real job is to transmit factual information grammatically. Think of translating legal documents, driving directions, or instructions on how to construct a harpsichord from a kit. Translating such texts is a matter of strict adherence to the (perceived) intended informational message of the original author. The translator can easily ignore the style of the original text without much threat of criticism. Instead of any of these types of texts, though, I'm going to choose poetry because the range of factors to consider is wider and because true facility in a second language entails recognition of these factors.

There are various types of poetry translations. Some of them are similar to the approach used in translating factual texts, such as instructions, in that they do not consider all of the factors present in the original. Let's look at an extreme case. The Austrian poet Ernst Jandl (1925–2000) focused on the importance of sound in poetry. He developed the art of "surface translation," whereby the sounds of a poem in one language would be rendered into another—using words native to the target language or nonsense words in the target language—without regard to meaning. When the two languages differ in their sound inventories (as most languages do), the closest approximation is acceptable. Here is an example of a poem in German by Rainer Maria Rilke, shown next to Jandl's surface translation into English. I've also provided a word-by-word translation so that you can see how the surface translation disregards the meaning of the words in the original poem.

Rilke's poem	Surface translation	Word-by-word
Der Tod ist groß.	Dare toadies gross	the death is big
Wir sind die Seinen	Vere sinned designing	we are the his
Lachenden Munds.	Laugh in the moons.	with laughing mouths
Wenn wir uns mitten	When we've ounce mitten	when we us midst
im Leben meinen	Am lay-by mine	in- in life believe
wagt er zu weinen	Farct hair so whining	dares he to cry
mitten in uns.	Midden in noons.	midst in us

I am not going to deal with surface translation of this sort but rather with holistic translation, which is more pertinent to second language learning.

Let's start by trying to translate a poem into English from a language that is quite similar to English—Dutch. Annette Hoeksema gave me this nursery rhyme, which Dutch children enjoy, and she translated each word individually for me:

Leentje leerde Lotje lopen
In de lange Lindenlaan
Maar toen Lotje niet wou lopen
Liet Leentje Lotje staan.

The very first word, *Leentje*, is a girl's name, as is the third word, *Lotje*. Do we leave them as is (in the Dutch) on the grounds that names can carry over from one language to another? That is, do you call your Italian friend Giuseppe and your Israeli friend Leila? Or should we choose English names, in the way in which you might call your Italian friend Joe and your Israeli friend Lilly?

The question may seem trivial, but it isn't. Our choice here might elicit emotional responses from the reader that we must be sensitive to. Let's say you have an Italian friend named Graziella. Do you call her Graziella or Grace? If you live in a city, probably neither choice seems very strange to you, and you'd be happy enough calling her Graziella. If you live in a small rural town, however, one where immigrants haven't been seen for generations, *Graziella* might seem to be a rather exotic name, one that could tend to isolate her from the community and one that you might even feel pretentious saying. We are trying to translate a nursery rhyme together, so maybe we want to stay away from anything that isolates the protagonists in the rhyme from the children who are reciting it and from anything that smacks of pretension.

All right, then, on the grounds that I want unpretentious names, I'm going to translate *Leentje* as 'Little Linda' and *Lotje* as 'Lottie.' You might object that in Dutch *Leentje* and *Lotje* both end in *tje*. So maybe these two names have something in common that should be preserved when we translate them. If you made this objection, you'd be right: The suffix *-tje* is a diminutive ending, comparable to the *-y* in *Johnny* and the *-ie* in *Bessie*. If we put the word *little* with one name but use the English diminutive *-ie* with the other, we lose this similarity between the names. So do we say *Lindy* and *Lottie* or *Little Linda* and *Little Lottie*? One problem with the second choice is that the diminutive is already present in *Lottie*, so having *little* as well seems unnecessary. On the other hand, maybe in your experience *Lindy* is unusual, making the first choice feel too exotic for a nursery rhyme. You might even want to substitute 'Lindsay' for *Lindy*.

How did we get into all this trouble just dealing with something so straightforward as proper names? Since there are many other issues for us to resolve as well, I'm simply going to translate the names as 'Lindy' and 'Lottie' and forge ahead.

Let's go to the other words in the first line: *Leerde* means 'taught' (it is marked for the past tense and for agreement with a third-person singular subject), and *lopen* is the infinitive (the completely tenseless form that has no agreement) for the verb *walk*. We can now translate the first line word for word:

Lindy taught Lottie walk

This isn't a grammatical sentence in English. I chose Dutch to start our investigation because it is so similar to English that word-by-word translations often yield grammatical results. I wanted our attempt at translation to be successful. We've hit a glitch here, though. The problem is with the verb *teach*. Several other verbs would have yielded a good sentence, for example:

Lindy {helped/let/made/watched/heard/saw} Lottie walk

However, for *teach* we need the extra word *to* in front of the verb *walk*. So let's translate the four words in line 1 of the Dutch nursery rhyme with an English line that consists of five words:

Lindy taught Lottie to walk

(Notice that many verbs behave like *teach* in requiring *to* before a following infinitive verb.)

Now let's go to the words in the second line: *In* means 'in,' *de* means 'the,' and *lange* means 'long.' The last word, *Lindenlaan*, is a proper name again, the name of a road. *Linden* has to do with linden trees, and *-laan* is translated as (and historically related to) our word *lane*. So let's say:

In the long Linden Lane

This has a fine sound to my ear (and it's because of how nicely Dutch translates into English that I chose it).

Let's move on to line 3. *Maar* means 'but,' *toen* means 'as/when,' *niet* means 'not,' *wou* means 'wanted' (again, past tense, third person), and *lopen* (again) means 'to walk.' If we translate word for word, we'll get the following:

But when Lottie not wanted walk

Again, the result is ungrammatical in English. English requires that *to* precede the infinitive verb *walk*, just as in line 1. English also requires another extra word because the negative *not* calls for an accompanying (helping or auxiliary) verb. (This did not used to be so, however; compare the biblical "Judge not lest ye be judged" to ordinary modern talk.) So let's put in the appropriate form of *do*:

But then Lottie did not want to walk

Read this line aloud. It's grammatical but stilted. In ordinary conversation we'd say *didn't* rather than *did not*. So maybe the line should be

> But when Lottie didn't want to walk

What can help us choose between these alternatives? Probably a consideration of our entire translation—the whole rhyme. However, for now let's take the line with the contraction (the ordinary line), and you can reevaluate later if you want.

In the final line, *Liet* means 'let' (past tense, third person, as with *leerde* and *wou*), and *staan* means 'stand.' A word-by-word translation yields

> Let Lindy Lottie stand

Trouble again: Do you even know what this line means? *Lindy* is the subject of the sentence here, so in English we'd rearrange the words to get

> Lindy let Lottie stand

Here's the first draft of our translation:

> Lindy taught Lottie to walk
> In the long Linden Lane
> But when Lottie didn't want to walk
> Lindy let Lottie stand

We are not done yet. Since this is a nursery rhyme in Dutch, we want it to be a nursery rhyme in English. Therefore, we need to see whether our translation has the characteristic elements of an English nursery rhyme. Nursery rhymes are often recognizable by their sound. Say our first draft aloud. Try to say the Dutch lines aloud (even though you are unsure of how to pronounce them).

Does our draft sound as much like a nursery rhyme as the Dutch does?

What are the sound elements of a nursery rhyme in English? One of them is rhyme itself. Dutch has a similar tradition. In the Dutch, the odd lines rhyme (actually, they end in the same word), as do the even lines. In our translation, the odd lines rhyme (and they end in the same word), but the even ones don't. So the English is a little off here.

Another sound element of nursery rhymes in English is the rhythm. Since most of my readers probably don't know Dutch (nor do I), you're going to have to believe me on this point: When Annette said the poem for me, each line had four strong beats (i.e., four obviously stressed syllables). The number of weak beats in each line, on the other hand, varied. The rules of rhythm in Dutch nursery rhymes, then, are a lot like those in English nursery rhymes. Consider this:

Thìrty dàys hàth Septèmber
Àpril Jùne ànd Novèmber

(Note that there is a strong beat on the first syllable of *April*.) The rule here is four strong beats to a line, but the number of weak beats doesn't matter. What kind of rhythmic pattern does our first draft of the translation have? A lot depends on how you say it aloud. As I read it, it has three strong beats in each line:

Lìndy taught Lòttie to wàlk
In the lòng Lìnden Làne
But when Lòttie didn't wànt to wàlk
Lìndy let Lòttie stànd

Shall we try to revise our translation to deal with these discrepancies? Let's take them one at a time. Certainly rhyme matters.

So let's try to revise the nursery rhyme so that lines two and four rhyme without losing the rhyme (here, identity) in lines one and three. I began by trying to find words that rhyme with *lane*, looking for one that would have a sense appropriate to the fourth line. I thought of *refrain*, not a word you'd expect in a nursery rhyme. No happy fit comes to my mind.

We could give up on keeping *lane* and look for two words that rhyme, one that is similar in meaning to *lane* and one that is similar in meaning to *stand*. I came up with *way* and *stay*. If we accept the rhyme *way/stay*, we give up the word *lane*. Does that bother you? Notice how many of the words in the Dutch poem begin with the letter "1." This alliteration will be reduced if we replace *lane* with *way*. On the other hand, *laan* in Dutch is not at the beginning of a word but rather is the second part of a compound word. So losing this alliteration is not so bad (perhaps), and now we will have a "w" alliteration, with the two instances of *walk*. Therefore, I vote for the *way/stay* rhyme.

Next, consider the rhythm. The Dutch line has one more strong beat than the English line. Do we want to make the English line longer perhaps? Or is this discrepancy acceptable? We have to be careful here because if we make the English line longer, we'll add words that don't correspond to anything in the Dutch line. On that basis alone, I vote to allow the discrepancy in rhythm.

Now, we've finally reached a point where our English translation sounds, at least to my ear, approximately like Annette's description of the Dutch original. Let's look at our final nursery rhyme revision:

> Lindy taught Lottie to walk
> In the long Linden Way
> But when Lottie didn't want to walk
> Lindy let Lottie stay

Perhaps we could do better than this, but I think that we've dealt with the major issues that this nursery rhyme offers. It's apparent that even something as simple as a nursery rhyme—and even translating between two languages as close as English and Dutch—offers serious challenges to the translator: Should significant or repeated elements of word structure (such as diminutives) be maintained? To what extent should the translation preserve elements of sound such as rhythm, rhyme, and alliteration? To what extent should the translation preserve style? At what point should conserving meaning be sacrificed and to what extent?

Let's look at translation from the other side—that is, a translation from English. Can you think of English utterances that present problems for a translator? What about

John kicked the bucket.

This is an idiom: It has a literal reading (one in which John slammed his foot against a bucket) and a figurative one (one in which John died). If *kicked the bucket* is not understood in the target language as meaning 'die,' how can we translate it to preserve the dual reading? Do we abandon kicking and buckets altogether and look for some analogous idiom in the target language?

Another question comes up when we think about how to translate a sentence such as this:

The dinner table was so festive, I expected him to serve turkey.

This is an English sentence, yet we know it is probably said by an American rather than an Australian, a Nigerian, or a South African. The turkey makes us think of the American Thanksgiving. It has that connotation, that cultural import. If someone were to translate this sentence into Chinese, would that person use the

Chinese word for turkey or pick some other food that was associated with a big family holiday in China? Certainly, the translator
could do either—and the choice might well depend on the purpose
of the translation. If this is part of a story about American life, the
translator would probably use a more literal translation. If this is
part of a story with a universal theme and if the setting of America
is not important, the translator might feel comfortable in using a
translation that was truer to the connotations of the sentence.

But how far do we go? What if we're dealing with allusions
rather than connotations? If there is a reference to Shakespeare
and we're translating into Italian, do we change it to a reference
to Dante? If we're translating into Russian, do we change it to a
reference to Pushkin?

Problems like idioms and connotations of certain vocabulary
items and allusions come up regardless of the languages you are
translating, and I'm sure you can think of many more. Consider
translating a passage into English that refers to an act of conversation. Do we use *chat, talk, discuss, converse, debate*, or something
else to denote that act? Formality, tone, and other matters of style
come into play regardless of the languages.

In fact, style is such an important part of translation that
sometimes styles develop in a language that are used only for
translated materials. For example, medieval Arabic translations of
ancient Greek philosophic texts were quite literal, often simply
word-by-word translations. This style wasn't used for other texts.
These stilted translations were then translated into Hebrew in the
1100s to 1300s, carrying that style with them. The result was a
special style of Hebrew used only for translation.

This situation may seem strange at first, but think about the
Bible. Many people object to modern renditions because they
believe that the earlier ones were truer to the language of the era.

However, some scholars say that the earlier renditions were stilted even for their times; in other words, they used a translation language rather than a smoothly flowing one. Ironically, the accuracy of a biblical translation is particularly thorny since the identity of the original manuscript is constantly under debate.

Sometimes problems come up between languages X and Y that wouldn't come up between languages X and Z. For example, the sentence

She has brothers

can be translated easily from English to Italian. However, if we try to translate it into Sanskrit, say, we'd need to know whether she had exactly two brothers or more than two. English makes the simple distinction of singular versus more than one (which is our plural), as do many languages, including Italian. However, Sanskrit makes the three-way distinction between singular, dual (precisely two), and more than two (which is their plural), as do certain other languages. Grammatical differences between languages, then, can introduce questions for the translator—sometimes questions the translator can't answer. Perhaps the sentence in question is in a passage that says nothing more about her brothers, so the translator does not know whether she has two or more than two. What should one do? If I were unable to confirm the precise information, I'd use the Sanskrit plural rather than the dual simply because the former is less precise (being any number greater than two). But I might, in fact, be wrong.

What all this means is that, before we can do a holistic translation of a text, we have to analyze it: We have to break it down into all the components that make it precisely what it is. Then we have to make judgment calls about how to render those components in the target language. Moreover, the target language might have differences in grammar that confound the translation, or it might belong to a culture that is different from the culture of the original language community in ways that again confound the translation. This analysis and this juggling act between grammars and cultures are part of every act of holistic translation, regardless of the languages. Compromises must be made, and the genius of translation lies, at least in part, in which compromises are made and how.

We can conclude, then, that translation is not a mechanical act; it doesn't proceed by any sort of simple algorithm. Rather, translation is a creative act. Some have even said that translating is rewriting. Different translators will offer different translations of the same text from language X into language Y. These different translations will have different strengths and drawbacks. Poetry, for example, involves meter, cadence, imagery, phrasing, and the personality of the voice of the poem. You might find you enjoy one translator's rendering of Dante's works more than another translator's. Does that mean that translations can be judged independently of the original? That they are perhaps as valuable as the originals? Some would say yes. Is one more (nearly) right than another? Or are all imperfect? Is true translation impossible to achieve, as some have argued?

One of the major flaws in the argument against the existence of true translations is the assumption that there is one correct way to interpret any text. Take something simple:

I love you.

This can be interpreted one way when a nurturing parent speaks to her child; another way when a parent is inducing guilt in her child; another way when a couple decides to marry; another way when that couple has been married for fifty years; another way when a prostitute says it to a stranger who's paying her to say it; another way when a teenager is trying to manipulate a girlfriend or boyfriend; another way when a child says it to a parent at the end of a long and wonderful day; and so on. If you and I went to a movie together and then discussed every line in the screenplay, we would undoubtedly have different interpretations of some of the lines—even though we both witnessed the same movie and were both aware of the contexts for all of them. We bring with us our experience about life and language when we interpret what we hear. Understanding language is a creative process.

So either we say it's impossible for us to truly understand each other even when we're speaking the same language, or we allow ourselves to enjoy the fluidity of our linguistic interactions—and thus to happily read all sorts of literature in translation. Furthermore, with this attitude we can study a second language with optimism. As speakers of a second language, we are constantly facing the issues that a translator encounters. This doesn't mean that we always need to be translating from our native tongue. If we become good enough at the second language, we will not consciously go through such an intermediate stage. What second language speakers share with the translator is the creative task of expressing something in the target language in a way that will be maximally effective.

Can we do it? Can we ever be proficient enough at a second language to express ourselves as effectively in it as in our native language? I know so many people who speak multiple languages magnificently well that I believe the answer is yes. But being equally effective does not mean being identical. Our experiences in one language community will always be different from our experiences in another one, and our experiences play a role in how we express ourselves.

Further Readings

Bialystok, E., ed. 1991. *Language processing in bilingual children*. New York: Cambridge University Press.

Brown, H. D. 1994. *Principles of language learning and teaching*, 2nd ed. Englewood Cliffs, N.J.: Prentice Hall Regents.

de Groot, A., and J. Kroll. 1997. *Tutorials in bilingualism: Psycholinguistic perspectives*. Hillsdale, N.J.: Erlbaum.

Ellis, R. 1985. *Understanding second language acquisition*. New York: Oxford University Press.

———. 1994. *The study of second language acquisition*. New York: Oxford University Press.

Flynn, S., and W. O'Neil. 1988. *Linguistic theory in second language acquisition*. Dordrecht: Kluwer.

Gardner, R., and W. Lambert, eds. 1972. *Attitudes and motivation in second language learning*. Rowley, Mass.: Newbury.

Hakuta, K. 1986. *Mirror of language: The debate on bilingualism*. New York: Basic Books.

Krashen, S. 1981. *Second language acquisition and second language learning*. Oxford: Pergamon.

Language acquisition. http://earthrenewal.org/secondlang.htm (May 3, 2009).

McLaughlin, B. 1987. *Theories of second language learning*. London: Arnold.

Schulte, R., and J. Biguenet, eds. 1992. *Theories of translation*. Chicago: University of Chicago Press.

Second language acquisition and children with visual and hearing impairments. http://www.tsbvi.edu/Outreach/seehear/spring00/secondlanguage.htm (accessed May 3, 2009).

Skehan, P. 1989. *Individual differences in second-language learning*. London: Arnold.

Tharp, R. G., and R. Gallimore. 1988. *Rousing minds to life: Teaching, learning, and school in social context*. New York: Cambridge University Press.

White, L. 1990. *Universal grammar and second language acquisition.*
    Amsterdam: Benjamins.

Further Reading on Translation

Bell, R., and C. Candin. 1991. *Translation and translating: Theory and
    practice.* Boston: Addison Wesley Longman.
Hatim, B., and I. Mason. 1990. *Discourse and the translator.* New York:
    Longman.
Larson, M. 1999. *Meaning-based translation: A guide to cross-language
    equivalence.* Lanham, Md.: University Press of America.
Newmark, P. 1991. *About translation.* Philadelphia: Multilingual Matters.
Shuttleworth, M., and M. Cowie. 1997. *Dictionary of translation studies.*
    Manchester, Eng.: St. Jerome.

Keywords

second language acquisition
translation

4 Does language equal thought?

An idea fundamental to cognitive science is that it may be possible to describe our thought processes through some representational system. Whether the appropriate representational system has properties similar to linguistic properties (such as observing similar principles) is an open question that scholars will no doubt be debating for years. Here, however, I'd like to address related questions, ones that I believe we can answer together: Do we think in language? Could we think without a language?

One way to interpret these questions is as follows: Does language construct a mental world that cognitively fences us in? This might well be a familiar question to you since it is frequently debated.

One can also interpret these questions in the most mundane way, the way people do when they say things such as "It's so noisy I can't hear myself think"—that is, asking whether human beings think in specific human languages. In other words, do people from Italy think in Italian? Or, given that the Italian language has many dialects, we could break down this basic question into multiple ones such as these: Do Venetians think in Venetian? Do Neapolitans think in Napoletano? Likewise, do Indians, Australians, Canadians, Americans, Nigerians, and the British think in their own national varieties of English? We can get nicer: Do Bostonians and Atlantans and Philadelphians think in their urban varieties? With either interpretation, the rest of this chapter aims to convince you that the answer to these questions is no.

I am first going to argue that thought does not require language by giving you instances of thought that couldn't possibly have been formulated in the brain in terms of language. The argument is a little long, so please keep that end point in sight.

Think about living with a toddler. Let me give you five scenarios that I've witnessed—three typical, two just plain wonderful—in which children did not use spoken or sign language. Then I bring out their relevance as a group to the central question of this chapter.

1. A boy plows a plastic truck across frozen grass. Another boy comes over, watches for a while, and then throws a handful of dirt on the first boy. The first boy picks up his truck, takes it to the area behind the swing set, and resumes plowing there.

2. My grandniece is coloring vehemently, and she rips the paper with the crayon. She takes another piece of paper, tapes it over the rip, and continues coloring.

3. A girl in the grocery store reaches for candy at the checkout aisle. Her mother says she can't have it. The girl throws a tantrum. Her mother's cheeks flame, and she gives the girl the candy.

4. Some three-year-olds sit in a line at the edge of a swimming pool, all of them with their feet dangling in the water. A man is teaching them to swim. He takes the first child on one end of the line and dunks him. That boy laughs. The instructor lifts him out of the pool, and the boy goes to the other end of the line. The instructor does the same to the next child, working his way along the line. My daughter, who is terrified of pools, is in the middle

of the line. When the instructor lifts the third child, my daughter reaches both hands into the pool, splashes herself, then runs to the end of the line—with the children who have already been dunked.

5. A boy goes to the beach with his family. The family on the next blanket has a blind child. The two children start digging together. At one point the mother of the first boy calls him over for a snack of carrot sticks. The boy takes his bag to the other boy and holds it out for him. When the blind boy doesn't react, the first boy takes the blind boy's hand (so beautifully covered with sand) and sticks it into the plastic bag. They share sandy carrots.

All of these scenarios give evidence of reasoning on the part of the child and, thus, of thought. Perhaps you disagree with me about one or another, but surely you agree about at least one. Now we are almost ready to approach the question of the relationship of thought to language in these types of scenarios.

But first let's consider one more situation. Consider the case of a hard-of-hearing or completely deaf child born to hearing parents. Often the fact that the child in this situation does not (adequately) hear is not detected until the child is a toddler or older. This is the case because the child exhibits behavior that is typical of toddlers—behavior precisely like that described in the preceding scenarios. That is, deaf children act just like hearing children in these sorts of situations. Yet deaf children whose deafness has not yet been discovered are linguistically deprived. Only after someone recognizes that these children don't hear can linguistic information be given to them—whether in the form of access to spoken language via hearing aids or cochlear implants, lessons in speech reading (what we used to call "lip-reading"), and/or lessons in vocaliza-tion or in the form of teaching the child (and often the whole family) to use sign language.

In other words, long before these deaf children have access to linguistic input, they do think, as is obvious from their thought-demonstrating behavior. There is no possibility, however, that their thought is in a specific human language since they have not even begun to acquire any specific human language.

A similar kind of argument can be made by looking at the studies of Genie, a young girl who was discovered in 1970 in Los Angeles, living in captive isolation that limited both her physical activity and linguistic input (also discussed in chapter 1). At the time of her discovery, she could hardly walk and gave no indica-tion of knowing what speech was. Several researchers worked for years to teach Genie language, and although she never progressed beyond an unsystematic stringing together of a few words, she did manage to talk about the events of her life, including events that had happened prior to her gaining linguistic knowledge. Clearly, these memories constitute thought—thought that was independent of linguistic structure.

Another way to argue that thought is not equivalent to spe-cific language is to consider our vocabulary. If a language has a word for a given concept and another language lacks a word for that concept, does it follow that the given concept is mentally accessible to people of the first language and inaccessible to people of the second? That is, do the two sets of speakers think differ-ently?

In answering this question, consider your own experiences in life. When you meet a new word, are you necessarily meeting a new concept? Let's say that I ask you to mix yellow and blue paints in varying amounts and put the different colors in a set of bowls.

Along the way, you happen to mix up chartreuse, but you don't know the particular word *chartreuse*. If I tell you that the mix in one bowl is called *chartreuse*, all I've done is given you a label. However, you already recognized the concept, or you wouldn't have put it in one of the bowls. That is, unless you are blind or color-blind, the actual qualities of the color precede your labeling of it. To take a more familiar example, in the United States, in voting booths many states have ballots that are punched by machine. The little parts that fall out of the ballot when it is punched are called chads. Before the presidential election of 2000, many Americans didn't know the word *chad*, but they were nevertheless familiar with the concept.

In these types of situations it seems rather obvious that the concept of an object can be understood without a word for that object, but what about a situation in which the concept concerns the identification not of a concrete object but rather of an abstract one?

Let me present two examples, contrasting English and Italian, as we consider whether the vocabulary difference between the two languages reveals a difference in thought possibilities. Italian lacks a vocabulary item corresponding to the English word *privacy*. Are we to conclude, then, that Italians do not understand the concept? Surely this is not a proper conclusion, and a simple observation of Italians' habits reveals this fact. Italians close the door when they use a public bathroom, they do not have sexual relations in public, and they do not ask personal questions of people they are not intimate with. In other words, they respect privacy regardless of the fact that they have no single word denoting that concept. So, although they will use a circumlocution to translate "Please respect my privacy," they understand the concept and communicate it effectively. Indeed, they have an adjective that is translated

as 'private'; they simply have a lexical gap (from an English perspective) when it comes to the relevant noun.

On the other hand, Italian has the word *scaramanzia*, for
which I know no single vocabulary item of English that can serve
as a translation. *Scaramanzia* is the superstition that makes us say
that the worst is going to happen in order to ward it off. For example, both my sisters had breast cancer, so I told my doctor (among
others) that I'm bound to get it. However, my fervent hope is
that I won't, and there's an ignorant but nonetheless real sense in
me that by saying I will get it, I've robbed that terrible evil of its
power. I've been doing things like that all my life, long before I had
ever heard the word *scaramanzia*. And now that I've described this
to you, I'm sure you understand the concept (which doesn't mean
that you share my ignorant attraction to magic), whether you've
ever practiced this behavior or not. Although most Italians and
Americans do not practice this behavior regularly, the fact that
people of both cultures understand the concept and occasionally
practice it shows that understanding the concept is independent of
having a vocabulary item in one's language that denotes it.

In sum, the presence and lack of the words *privacy* and *scaramanzia* in Italian and English tell us nothing whatsoever about
differences between the ways English speakers and Italian speakers
think.

Analogous arguments can be made by looking at vocabulary
differences in any two languages. German has the word *Schadenfreude*, which is a compound of the root for 'damage' and the root
for 'joy.' *Schadenfreude* is the pleasure one takes in the misfor-
tunes of others. Although you might not have experienced this
pleasure, nor might many Germans, you can understand the concept regardless of the fact that English has no such word. Often
the villains in soap operas and the like are more hateful because

we recognize that they experience *Schadenfreude*. One language will coin a word for a given concept, whereas another language will not. Scholars of various disciplines (psychology, sociology) might debate the reasons for this, but the important point for us is simply that the speakers of both languages can understand the concept, regardless.

You might argue that the existence of a word for a concept in a given language in some way legitimizes or licenses the concept in that linguistic community. That is, we have a word for it, so the concept must be shared by many and is, therefore, somehow more true or real than it might be without a linguistic label. This could be right. Nevertheless, the licensing of a concept is distinct from the ability to grasp it. In the college where I work, many first-year students enter with the fear that our highly selective admissions committee made a mistake and they don't belong here. We have no single word for this fear (which is shared by first-year students on many campuses, no doubt), but it's easy to recognize and understand.

Vocabulary differences are not the only differences between languages, so we should turn now to other types of differences and ask what they tell us about the relationships between language and thought. Some scholars have argued that a certain population cannot reason in the same way as another population because of syntactic differences between the languages of the two populations. Instead of reporting on that literature (which would require a lengthy discussion), I'll present an analogous situation that has not been widely discussed in this light. We will look again at a contrast between Italian and English, this time focusing on sentence structure.

In English we can say, "John beat the eggs stiff," meaning that John beat the eggs with the result that they became stiff. The word *stiff* in this sentence is called a resultative secondary predicate. In

Romance languages the literal translation of that sentence is not grammatical because Romance languages do not allow resultative secondary predicates in as wide a range of sentence structures as English does. Instead, in a Romance language you'd say something that would be translated literally as 'John beat the eggs until they became stiff' or 'John beat the eggs to the point of (their) being stiff.' A person who holds to the idea that thought is language might try to use this information to argue that Italians, Spaniards, Romanians, French, Portuguese, and speakers of other Romance languages cannot understand the concept of direct result. But that's obviously false. Speakers of Romance languages clearly understand the concept of direct result; they simply have available a different range of sentence structures to render it.

Analogous arguments can be built around other sentence structure differences between languages. For example, some languages express possession by a verb that can be translated as 'have.' Others, however, express it in other ways, such as by stating existence with respect to something else. For example, to express 'I have a sister' in Russian, one would say *u menja sestra*. A word-by-word translation of this is 'with-me-sister.' (Note that there is no verb here. Typically the verb that means 'be' is omitted when the present tense is to be conveyed.) Does that mean that the speakers of the first type of language (including English) have a different sense of possession from the speakers of the second type of language (including Russian)? In particular, do we think of sisters differently? At a certain point, the proposition that structural differences between languages are evidence of differences in conceptual behavior between peoples leads to nonsense. In my opinion, this is one of those times.

Another argument that language and thought are not equivalent comes from the fact that we can speak without thinking. We do it much too often, are surprised at what we have said, and then correct it. In fact, we can even read without thinking, coming to the end of the page and realizing that we have no idea what we've just read. Sometimes we can read aloud, thus indisputably using our language mechanism, and still think about something else, so that we lose our place in the passage and don't even know what we've read and what we haven't. Similarly, if you've ever heard particularly verbal preschoolers speak, you'll be amazed by their fluency and ability to express even abstract concepts, for example when talking about future events. In the following sentence, for instance, uttered by a three-year-old boy whose grandfather lives in a different country and only gets to visit him once or twice a year, the boy expresses something about a future event, without really having a concept of time: "I'm putting all these things in a bag for grandpa because when he comes and we fix the bench together, we need this." A moment later, the boy could be throwing a tantrum about not being able to go to the playground right that moment but having to wait until a little later, demonstrating that future events are hard for him to integrate into his thinking. It is obvious, then, that preschoolers' reasoning ability lags far behind their speaking ability. This is particularly striking evidence that language (whether in the form of speaking or reading) and thought cannot be one and the same, nor are they even necessarily dependent on each other.

Many more arguments can be brought to bear on the question of whether thought equals language. We could ask whether animals think, and if our answer is positive (as mine is), we must abandon the notion that thought is language since animals do not have language in the sense that humans do (a point discussed in chapter 6). We could ask whether people who have brain disease or injury that robs them of language still think, and if our answer is positive, we must again abandon this notion. However, even without looking at the vast amount of research on animals and on language pathologies, that is, without looking at research that goes beyond our daily experience, we can debunk certain myths about language simply by looking at the evidence available in everyday life. The myth that we think in specific languages is one of those debunkable myths, as we've already seen.

This conclusion does not minimize the importance of the various relationships that hold between language and thought. Language facilitates the introduction and transmission of thoughts, and a particular phrasing of a concept can give it a slant that offers the listener a new perspective. Sometimes we may not even be quite sure of our thoughts until we put them into language, which is one reason that talking to a confidant when making crucial decisions can be so valuable. Speaking one's mind or writing one's ideas can also help one to recognize the form of a particular rational argument one is developing. Using language can help us in analysis of many types, just as drawing what we saw can help us understand its significance. Nonetheless, the drawing is not tantamount to the act of seeing; likewise, expressing oneself in language is not tantamount to the act of thinking.

Language is like a hanger that we put our thoughts on. When the clothing is in a pile on the floor, it might be harder to recognize it for what it truly is. The structure of the hanger clarifies the structure of the clothing, but clarification of an essence is distinct from the essence itself.

In sum, whether or not we have words for concepts, we can and do entertain those concepts, and some concepts we may never have words for—because they are ineffable.

I want to close with a final consideration, which again connects to daily experience—one I'd simply like to pose. Observe the following conversation between two speakers:

I hate snakes.

Do you remember Mrs. Bicknell?

Our eighth-grade social studies teacher?

Yes.

Sure, I remember her. Why?

Well, when you said snakes, I remembered the day I went to
     talk to her after school about how my family was falling
     apart, and she asked me what the matter was and if
     Patrick had walked some other girl home, and she was
     so condescending that I just left and walked home alone
     and saw this twisted stick by the sidewalk, and I said,
     "You look like a crazy snake. Hello, you crazy snake."
     I thought I was alone, but Patrick was walking right
     behind me, and he said, "I always thought you were
     crazy, but now I know."

Oh.

When the second speaker goes into that long speech, you can see
how much thought she's reporting—thought that apparently took
place between the first utterance ("I hate snakes.") and the second
("Do you remember Mrs. Bicknell?") If all of that thought took
place in actual English sentences, it would have had to come at a
remarkable speed. In addition, although the production of English
in this long thought between the first and the second utterance
would be free of speech production—and thus free of the slow-
ness of the speech articulators (the tongue, the lips, the bottom
jaw, and all the other parts of the body that participate in speech
production)—it is still a stream of silent words, which if spoken
would come as fast as a voice recording increased to a continu-
ous squeak. The speed of thought exceeds that of speech, of the
fastest fingers typing, and even of a brief, meaningful look. Can

silent language possibly be that fast? Ideally, we should design an experiment to measure the speed of silent language at this point. If we cannot do that, if we cannot devise some way to test whether or not silent language has the characteristics of thought (such as great speed), we are left in an unsupported position.

But even without experimental evidence, we can push the hypothesis—that language and thought are equivalent—to an absurd end by considering the language and thought of Deaf people (by *Deaf* with a capital "D," I mean people whose primary language is a sign language) with regard to speed. Signs generally take about twice as long to produce as words. So do Deaf people think twice as slowly as hearing people (since they would be thinking in visual signs)? Moreover, some Deaf people have mastered spoken languages. I have such friends, and they speak English at the ordinary rate. So do these Deaf people think at double the rate when they are speaking as when they are signing? The proposal, again, is nonsensical to me.

Thought is thought. Language is language. The two are distinct.

Further Reading

Carruthers, P., and J. Boucher, eds. 1998. *Language and thought: Interdisciplinary themes*. New York: Cambridge University Press.

Chomsky, N., and R. Anshen. 1995. *Language and thought*. Wakefield, R.I.: Moyer Bell.

Fauconnier, G. 1997. *Mappings in thought and language*. New York: Cambridge University Press.

Gauker, C. 1994. An essay on the relation between thought and language. Princeton: Princeton University Press.

Gumperz, J., and S. Levinson, eds. 1996. *Rethinking linguistic relativity*. New York: Cambridge University Press.

Li, P., and L. Gleitman. 2002. Turning the tables: Language and spatial reasoning. *Cognition* 83: 265–94.

Papafragou, A., C. Massey, and L. Gleitman. 2002. Shake, rattle 'n' roll: The representation of motion in language and cognition. *Cognition* 84: 189–219.

Stanford Encyclopedia of Philosophy. The language of thought hypothesis. http://plato.stanford.edu/entries/language-thought/ (accessed May 3, 2009).

Vygotsky, L., and A. Kozulin. 1986. *Thought and language*. Cambridge, Mass.: MIT Press.

Keywords

language and thought
linguistic determinism

5 Are sign languages real languages?

Almost all hearing people have seen Deaf people communicating with each other by moving their hands, heads, and torsos either on television or in real life. The manual-visual language they are using is called *sign language*. Many hearing children know the manual alphabet used by Deaf people in America, and many hearing children and adults can make a few signs, but most hearing people do not have Deaf friends.

You might object to that last claim because you are a hearing person and you have a friend who has been losing or has already lost his hearing as he grew older. So I want to make a distinction between people whose first language is a spoken language and who lose their hearing through injury, disease, or aging and, most important, who never use a sign language as their major means of communication—who are typically called deaf people (with a small "d")—and people who are hard of hearing or cannot hear at all (for whatever reason) and who use a sign language as their major means of communication—who are called Deaf people (with a capital "D," indicating a cultural group as opposed to an audiological status). People in the first group are integrated into hearing society; people in the second group are generally not.

Again, you might object to that last claim, but let me give you a point of comparison. Looking at figures from 2002, we estimate that there are about 24 million deaf or hard-of-hearing people in the

United States, of which a significant percentage are Deaf—estimates range up to around 3 million, although it may be more like 2 million (see the Gallaudet Research Institute figures on demographics at http://www.gri.gaulladet.edu). Compare these figures to those for Jewish Americans: There are at most around 6 million Jewish people in the United States, fewer than half of whom claim synagogue membership (see the Jerusalem Center for Public Affairs figures on demographics at http://www.jcpa.org). So there might be about the same number of Deaf people as there are synagogue members in the United States. Yet many people who are not members of synagogues have Jewish friends who are members of synagogues. In contrast, very few hearing people have Deaf friends. Simply put, Deaf people in America are part of a separate culture from hearing people.

Why? The answer to this question is going to be long and involves answering the main question of this chapter—that is, whether or not sign languages are real languages. Furthermore, since access to language is not just a basic human right but also the means by which so many of our civil rights are delivered, the fact that many deaf and hard-of-hearing people have experienced at least partial blockage to language access (particularly access to the language of a majority culture) means that they have experienced a curtailment of rights. For this reason, this chapter also dips into the relationship between language and civil rights.

I'd like you to gather nine friends (plus you, to make a total of ten) who do not sign and play a game that is similar to charades. Give each friend a numbered index card with a sentence on it, such as the following:

1. I'm scared.
2. You're tall.

   3. He's mean.
   4. Let's swim.
   5. I'm hungry.
   6. That lion is happy.
   7. Where's the dog?
   8. How did you do that?
   9. Why do you think Marilyn Monroe got mixed up with JFK?
  10. What did your aunt say last Tuesday when you confessed you lost her entire life savings at the racetrack?

Now, going in order of the numbers on the cards, each person should do whatever is necessary to make the others guess the sentence on the card without saying or mouthing any words. (If you hate the idea of using friends, try doing it yourself in front of a mirror.) It is likely that the game will be easy at first and get increasingly difficult as you go through the numbered sentences. Notice how simple sentences 7 and 8 are yet how difficult it is to communicate them without language. Sentences 9 and 10 should leave you at a loss.

Have a discussion with your friends about why some of the sentences were easier to guess than others. Pointing makes talking about *I* or *you* or *he* (if he's present) quite easy. However, you can't use pointing alone to talk about *that lion* or *the dog* or *Marilyn Monroe* or *JFK* or *your aunt*. Ideas in the words *scared, mean, happy, tall*, and *swim* are relatively easy to transmit by making facial expressions, raising your hand, or mimicking swimming motions, but it's more difficult to use such simple methods to indicate the ideas in the words *where, how, why, mixed up, confessed, think, say*, and so on. Moreover, how do you act out time frames, especially points in time as particular as last Tuesday?

The information in all of those English sentences can easily be conveyed in sign language. In fact, any sentence in English or any other spoken language can be conveyed in sign language. Sign languages can communicate information about people and objects that are not present (so they can't be pointed to), about specific times (in the past, in the future, and now), and about very particular events (such as forgetting to buy the candles the kindergarten teacher asked you to pick up). Think about what this means concerning the relationship between the structural form of an individual sign and its meaning. For most signs, that relationship must not be predictable; in fact, it must be arbitrary.

The last sentence might strike you as strange, but think about spoken language. Why do English speakers call a chicken a chicken? Why do we call shoes shoes? There is nothing about the sound of the word *chicken* or the sound of the word *shoes* that makes us able to guess their meaning. If languages worked in such a way, we might be able to guess the meaning of most words in most languages, but we can't. Can you guess the meaning of the Chinese word *jia* ('chicken')? Can you guess the meaning of the Italian word *scarpe* ('shoes')? For any given word in any spoken language, the correspondence between sound and meaning is typically arbitrary because for most words no other possibility arises.

The kinds of words that would be open to a nonarbitrary correspondence between meaning and sound are those whose meaning has to do with sound. When we say that a bee buzzes, we might think that the meaning of the word *buzz* sounds like the actual word, and so we might feel that there's a predictable correspondence between meaning and sound. Such words are called onomatopoetic. Actually, though, if you look at the English words whose meanings are sounds (especially words that mean the noises animals make, like *meow* or *moo* or *cock-a-doodle-doo*), you will find that their counterparts in other languages are often (probably jusually) not recognizable. In fact, when speakers of one language are asked to guess at the meaning of so-called onomatopoetic words in other languages, their guesses vary widely. Thus, the whole idea of onomatopoeia is questionable (and linguists debate it, often modifying the notion in subtle and sensible ways in order to capture generalizations—that is, in some languages certain classes of words identified by sound characteristics behave in predictable ways, and we need a way to recognize that grammatical fact).

However, even if you believe that some words are onomatopoetic, it's clear that most are not and could not be because the meaning of most words is not concerned with particular sounds. In studies in which linguists have asked people why a given word means what it does, the people can't answer. The very question is a puzzle because language is not organized to have a predictable correspondence between sound and meaning, and we know this fact even if we've never explicitly discussed it. In one study, a bowl of spaghetti was put in front of a Canadian speaker of English. He was asked why he called it spaghetti. He looked at the linguist, baffled. Then he said something to this effect: "It looks like spaghetti. It smells like spaghetti." He took a bite. "It *is* spaghetti."

Therefore, we can feel more comfortable with the fact that the relationship between the structure of a sign and its meaning is for the most part arbitrary. Sign languages are like spoken languages in that their vocabulary is characterized as having an arbitrary relationship between form (whether a manual structure or sounds) and meaning.

Although this fact is utterly natural, given everything you know about language, many people have trouble believing it. It is not uncommon to find assumptions or even outright claims to the contrary—essentially, claims that signs are iconic. Iconicity is as impossible for most signs as onomatopoeia is for most words. To see that, we need to know what the structure of a sign is.

Hold out your dominant hand (the one you write with). Since most of us are right-handed, I assume that you have your right hand out now—so, if you are left-handed, make the necessary changes in what follows. Straighten all of your fingers and your palm, and keep all of the fingers close beside one another except for the thumb. Now hold this flat hand in front of your ribs, with the palm facing down and the fingertips facing away from the body. Move your wrist from the center of your body to the side of your body (if your right hand is extended, you are moving it from left to right), so that your flat hand hits a starting point and then lightly bounces in the air to an ending point. (It's as though you pat one place in the air, then raise your hand and move it over simply by a movement of the wrist, and pat a second place in the air.) If my directions are good enough, you've made the American Sign Language (ASL) sign CHILDREN (signs are always written in small capitals, by convention).

(If you have access to the Web, you might want to go to an ASL dictionary and view the sign. I recommend the site http://commtechlab.msu.edu/sites/aslweb/. But, in case you cannot access the Web now, I will continue describing signs.)

Now do the same movement (bouncing from left to right) of that same flat hand but this time with the palm facing up. You've made the ASL sign SOMETHING. Thus, the orientation of the palm matters in distinguishing one sign from another.

Now hold both hands in front of you, palms touching each other, with the right (the dominant) palm facing down and the other facing up. Keep the palms touching as you hold the left hand stationary, and move the right hand with that same flick of the wrist from left to right. (You can't bounce the top hand here since it stays in contact with the bottom hand.) You've made the ASL sign CHEESE. (Actually, in isolation this sign typically involves repetition of the wrist motion, but in quick conversation, just one flick of the wrist can do.) Therefore, where you move the dominant hand (in front of your ribs or on top of your other hand) matters. In other words, the place a sign is made matters in distinguishing one sign from another.

Now move your dominant hand back in front of your ribs, and face this flat palm downward again. Move the wrist—but this time move it so that the tips of the fingers go up and down. You've made the ASL sign BOUNCE. Movement matters in distinguishing one sign from another.

Now keep your dominant hand in front of your ribs, palm downward, and do the old movement of the wrist from side to side with the same bounce you did for CHILDREN. This time, though, stick out straight only your thumb, index finger, and middle finger, all three spread, and let your two last fingers curl under. You've made the ASL sign THIRTY-THREE. Thus, the handshape matters in distinguishing one sign from another.

From looking at just five different signs, we can see that four parameters are important in talking about the structure of a sign: palm orientation, location, movement, and handshape. There are other parameters of signs as well, but consideration of just these four is adequate for our discussion.

We are still investigating the issue of iconicity in sign languages. If a sign were to be iconic, there would have to be a nonarbitrary relationship between its structure and its meaning. Because we typically view structure in a sign language (as we hear structure in a spoken language), the sign would have to look like what it meant. That is, somehow the combination of parameters that make up a sign would have to look like the meaning of the sign. What kinds of signs, then, even have the potential to be iconic? These are signs whose meanings have to do with physical objects whose shape the hand(s) can reasonably assume and/or with a stance or movement that the hands can reasonably mimic.

Hold out your dominant hand again. Extend the index and middle fingers straight and spread, and curl the other three under so that the thumb tip closes over the other two fingertips. If you held this handshape in front of you with the palm facing out and the extended fingertips facing up, you would have the V sign for victory in ordinary gestures. Now give the nondominant hand the same flat handshape we used in the first five signs. Point the extended fingertips of the dominant hand downward so that they rest on the palm of the nondominant hand. You have made the sign STAND. See how the two extended fingers look like a person's legs standing on the nondominant palm? If you now bend the extended fingers so they lose contact with the nondominant palm and then extend them, making contact again, you've made the sign JUMP (at least as it appears in many ASL dictionaries). In addition, if you bend them and make contact with the nondominant palm while the extended fingers are bent so that the knuckles are on the palm, you've made the sign KNEEL.

These sorts of signs seem about as close to iconic as signs can get, but let's do the same kinds of tests that I talked about for onomatopoeia. Make the sign KNEEL, and ask people who don't know any ASL what it means. When I do that with my students, their responses vary a great deal, but if I show them the sign STAND and tell them what it means and then I show them the sign KNEEL, they can usually guess correctly. So it's really only once the analogy is pointed out to them (between the two active fingers and the legs of a person) that they can use whatever degree of iconicity there is in these signs to figure out the meaning. Furthermore, if you look at the counterparts to these signs in other sign languages around the world, it won't be easier to guess what they mean than it is to guess the meaning of so-called onomatopoetic words in spoken languages. In other words, if iconicity exists at all in sign languages, it affects only a tiny part of the vocabulary.

You can convince yourself of the fact that the vocabulary of sign languages has an arbitrary correspondence between structure and meaning just by looking at any two Deaf people who are signing together. If signs were truly iconic, we'd be able to guess the meaning of a conversation without knowing the sign language at all. But we can't.

There's another point to be made here as well. Sometimes when a sign is first coined, it has a high degree of iconicity, but over time signs often lose that iconicity, particularly if the iconicity conflicts with phonological principles. Let me give you two examples. The sign JUMP described earlier is common to many signers. However, many native signers make JUMP with a bent V handshape the entire time. That is, they don't alternate handshapes between the V with extended fingers and the V with curled fingers. (Change of handshape within a sign is phonologically disfavored.) This sign can no longer be seen as strictly iconic, for if it were, it would indicate bouncing on one's knees! A second example involves the sign TAPE RECORDER. Originally both hands were extended in front of the chest with the index fingers pointing straight ahead and the rest of the fingers curled under, while the two index fingers made parallel clockwise circles in the air on an imaginary vertical wall in front of the signer. However, after a number of years, the sign changed: Now the right hand makes a clockwise circle, while the left hand makes a counter-clockwise circle. (Reflexive symmetry across a midsaggital plane is phonologically favored.) But any tape recorder that worked this way would instantly snap the tape.

These examples show not only that iconicity is lost over time, but also that sign languages, like spoken languages, change over time. Importantly for our discussion, the ways in which isolated lexical items change phonological shape (the phonological shape of a sign is seen in the four parameters) is determined by phonological rules or principles in sign languages, just as in spoken languages. So historical evidence also verifies the bona fide status of sign languages.

Neurolinguistics adds fuel to the fire. Brain imaging has shown us that sign language comprehension is accompanied by substantial neuronal activity in the left hemisphere of the brain and in precisely those same areas that are activated in the comprehension of spoken languages. In other words, language is language, whether the modality is oral/aural or manual/visual. Interestingly, in native signers (as opposed to signers who learn to sign after the onset of puberty), not only is the left hemisphere activated, but the right hemisphere is as well. This is not a surprising find, given the fact that vision involves right hemisphere activity, but it is pertinent to our discussion because it indicates that sign languages have a critical period for learning right around the onset of puberty, just as spoken languages do. Anyone who learns to sign after that period will sign nonnatively (although they may, of course, sign fluently and extremely well—just as late learners of a spoken language can be excellent, though nonnative, speakers).

Now I want to end with one final point about signing, which I hope will not confound the previous conclusion. Although individual signs are not iconic, often in signing a conversation a certain amount of drawing in the air takes place. Let's say that someone wants to sign the sense of the sentence "I was driving along, and I saw flames shooting out of a tall apartment building on my left, so I stopped and ran across the street into a pharmacy to get help." As part of signing this, she will probably indicate a building with apartments on the left side of the signing space in front of her and point to the top of that building before she makes the sign for flames. She will also probably move her finger from that apartment building to the right side of the signing space in front of her to indicate that the pharmacy is directly across the street from the apartment building. She might use the sign RUN, or she might move her finger quickly to the position in the signing space that she has set up for the pharmacy (or both). These parts of signing the sentence—indicating relative position and the type of movement by going slowly or quickly—are similar to drawing in the air. It's no surprise that sign language does this because sign is received visually.

Because of facts like these, sign language linguists often make a distinction between frozen lexical items (the kind you find in a dictionary) and productive ones (the kind you create in conversation for expressing specific actions, as exemplified in the preceding paragraph). The productive part is still symbolic (as all language is), but that symbolism is more nearly transparent in that the productive part locates points in the air, establishing analogies with locations in the real world, and then indicates activity involving those points, where the action of the articulators (the hands, arms, head, torso) is metaphorical with regard to the action in the real world.

In sum, sign languages are real languages—they are not merely unstructured gestures, nor are they iconic. So learning to sign and to understand any sign language is similar to learning to speak and to understand any spoken language.

We will return to matters concerning Deaf people, sign languages, and civil rights in chapter 12.

Further Readings

American Sign Language Browser. http://commtechlab.msu.edu/sites/
    aslweb/browser.htm (accessed May 3, 2009).

Aronoff, M., I. Meir, and W. Sandler. 2005. The paradox of sign language
    morphology. *Language* 81: 302–44.

Bornstein, H., ed. 1990. *From manual communication: Implications for
    education.* Washington, D.C.: Gallaudet University Press.

Cohen, H. 1994. *Train go sorry: Inside a Deaf world.* Boston, Mass.:
    Houghton Mifflin.

Klima, E., U. Bellugi, and R. Battison. 1979. *The signs of language.*
    Cambridge, Mass.: Harvard University Press.

Kyle, J., and B. Woll, eds. 1983. *Language in sign.* London: Croom Helm.

———. 1985. *Sign language: The study of Deaf people and their language.*
    New York: Cambridge University Press.

Messing, C. 1999. *Gestures, speech, and sign.* New York: Oxford
    University Press.

Neidle, C., J. Kegl, D. MacLaughlin, B. Bahan, and R. Lee. 1999.
    *The syntax of American Sign Language: Functional categories and
    hierarchical structure.* Cambridge, Mass.: MIT Press.

Newman, A., D. Bavelier, D. Corina, P. Jezzard, and H. J. Neville. 2002.
    A critical period for right hemisphere recruitment in American
    Sign Language processing. *Nature Neuroscience* 5: 76–60.

Stokoe, W. 1960. *Sign language structure: An outline of visual
    communication systems of the American Deaf.* Silver Spring, Md.:
    Linstok.

———. 1965. *A dictionary of American Sign Language on linguistic
    principles.* Silver Spring, Md.: Linstok.

Wilbur, R. 1979. *American Sign Language and sign systems.* Baltimore:
    University Park Press.

Keywords

sign language
signed versus spoken languages

6 Do animals have language?

You may have heard of Koko, the gorilla, or you may have read about bee dances. Many people, including some biologists, think that these examples show that animals have language. One of the biggest issues in this question is determining exactly what language is. I began an informal investigation, surveying a variety of people on the definition of *language*. The first person I asked kept returning to the notion of the passing of information. Undoubtedly, some instances of language involve the passing of information, but let's say I find that a branch has fallen off the big, old silver maple in my front yard, exposing a core of rot. I now know that my tree is sick. Information has been received, but did an event of language occur? Surely not, as my tree does not use language. So the passing of information cannot be sufficient grounds for calling an event an instance of language.

Someone else talked about communication but with a different slant. She talked about a sense of purpose—about communication in which the source intends to send a message. Again, there's no doubt that language can be a type of purposeful communication, but let's say I'm sick of the mess in my son's bedroom, so I sweep it all together into a giant pile that blocks the entrance to his room. When he comes home, he puts everything away where it should go. I sent a message; he received it. Communication occurred—and on purpose. However, sweeping his junk into a pile is not an instance of language. We have myriad ways to communicate, many of which do not involve language, and this is one of them.

What, then, do you know about language? You might respond that it involves sounds, and spoken language certainly does, but we write to each other, and we sign to each other as well, so not all language instances involve sounds. Furthermore, we can make many sounds that aren't part of language. Sound is neither necessary nor sufficient for an event of language to occur.

You know a lot about language.

Why, for instance, is:

the into runs sweetlying never clouds

not an utterance you might expect to hear? How is it different from other unusual utterances, like this famous one by Noam Chomsky:

Colorless green ideas sleep furiously.

Both utterances are nonsense, but the first one is really much worse. It's wrong in more ways than the second one, which seems to be a well-formed sentence structurally, although it simply makes no sense. The first one isn't even anything we'd call a sentence.

The description of a language, what linguists call a grammar, involves the explicit statement of many rules. There are various types of rules—rules about sound and word formation, as well as sentence structure and meaning—and we apply them without conscious knowledge that we are doing so. However, we easily recognize when the rules are violated. The first nonsense utterance—*the into runs sweetlying never clouds*—is terrible because a variety of rules for word structure, sentence structure, and meaning are violated, whether or not you can state precisely which rules are involved. I could have made the same point by using analogous examples from any human language in the world, including any sign language (but I would have had to provide a video of someone demonstrating nonsense signs). A grammar, then, is a collection of rules that describes a language, and a grammar is a definitional part of what makes something a language.

What else do you know about language? In the first nonsense utterance, there is something wrong with the position of *the*. A preposition follows it, and in English *the* shouldn't be followed by a preposition. Also, the word *clouds* is too far away from *the*. Whatever specific thing you noticed, you know that the position of *the* is somehow wrong. Did anyone ever teach you the rules for the position of *the* in an English sentence? If you are a native speaker of English, you simply knew. You learned it on your own without anyone explicitly teaching you. This is another one of the important facts about language: We have the ability to acquire it without any formal instruction. We are set up, hard-wired, to learn it. This is another definitional part of language—its innateness (see chapter 1 for more information).

Consider the range of things that you can say, such as a sentence like this:

> Hey, kids, your mother left last night, but don't worry, she'll be back when she's come to terms with the whole notion of mortality.

(This was said tongue in cheek by a friend, but it's a useful example.) By uttering certain sounds in a given order, the speaker of this sentence is addressing particular individuals (the kids), referring to a particular individual who isn't there (their mother), referring to times that are not the present (last night and whenever the mother comes to terms), and referring to abstract ideas (worry and mortality). The ability to refer to things that are not physically present (objects here, and times) is known as displacement. Both displacement and the ability to refer to abstractions are common to all human languages.

Now consider this sentence:

> To make a really good pasta with pesto, you need to buy
> a type of flat, long pasta that is just a little wider than
> linguine—called trenette—and when the pasta is almost
> finished being boiled, you have to add string beans (thin
> ones—or else cut them lengthwise in half) and very thinly
> sliced potatoes to the pot.

The person hearing this utterance might well choose to go shopping for trenette, string beans, and potatoes, but we would not expect the person to head for the hardware store or go outside and dig a fishpond. Under normal conditions, humans associate meaning with words and sentences and show this by reacting in ways that are typically neither random nor simply reflexes.

Finally, there are plenty of sentences in this chapter that you've never read or heard before. Human language is creative; it allows us to express novel ideas rather than simply repeating a closed set of utterances. Following morphological rules, we can recombine the meaningful units of words (morphemes) and create new words (for example, *demousify* if you need to rid your house or shed of mice), and following syntactic rules, we can recombine words and create new sentences (for example, the sentence you're reading right this moment).

There are more things we could say about language, but these six are enough to help us determine whether the following instances of animal behavior are evidence of language of the type found among humans. So we'll be looking for evidence of

1. rules that might constitute a grammar
2. innateness
3. displacement
4. the ability to refer to abstractions
5. the existence of meaningful units (such as words) as evidenced by appropriate behavior on the part of listeners
6. the ability to create novel language expressions

Research on animal language has included the study of bees, birds, sea mammals, and various primates. Some of these studies deal with pheromones, scents involved primarily in sexual behavior. In this chapter I'm going to look at other types of phenomena that potentially offer better candidates for language status. Observations of bees have shown that honeybee communities send out scouts to look for food. When food is located, the scouts return to the hive and recruit other bees to help them bring back the food. First, the recruiter gives the others a sample of the food, so they'll know their goal. Next, the recruiter performs a dance that identifies the location of the food. The dance can have two shapes: The "round" dance is circular and is used when the food is within one hundred meters of the hive; the "wagging" dance involves a stretched-out figure eight and is used when the food is farther away. The rate at which the bee does the wagging dance conveys the distance to the food source; the farther it is, the slower the bee dances. Finally, the vigor of the waggle indicates the quality of the food.

Distance is not the only information needed; the bees also have to know the direction to the food source. With the round dance, there seems to be no indication of direction, perhaps because the short distance makes it less important. With the wagging dance, however, direction is indicated by the orientation of the bee's head. The hive is typically vertical. If the top of the hive is taken to be coincidental with the location of the sun, and if the bee faces straight ahead when performing the dance, the food source lies directly below the sun. If the bee's head is angled sixty degrees off the vertical, for example, then the food is located at a sixty-degree angle from the sun.

The dances of four species of honeybees have been studied so far, and in three of those species the dancing bee produced a low-frequency sound that seems to be essential in conveying the information. These three species perform their dance in the light or in the dark; that is, they do not have to have optimal visual circumstances. The one species that is silent during the dance always performs in daylight. Thus, sound might well be adding information in cases in which the bees might miss visual information.

The bees who witness the dance generally arrive at the food source without much difficulty, but sometimes there are problems. If a barrier lies between the hive and the food source, the recruiter bee cannot give directions around it. Instead, the other bees fly in a straight path toward the food source; when they meet the barrier, they typically fly up and over it even if the path the recruiter bee flew in returning to the hive was shorter. Eventually they learn shortcuts on their own. Also, if the hive has fallen or been knocked askew so that the combs are not vertical, the recruiter bee will orient the dance as though the representation of the sun is the actual direction of the sun rather than the top of the hive. However, if the hive is in a dark enclosure, as when scientists put it in a box for experimental purposes, the dance is ineffective in conveying information about the location of the food.

Although this description is brief and incomplete, the gist should be apparent. Given this, is the bee dance a form of language? It certainly has rules (as in 1), exhibits displacement in referring to food sources that aren't present (as in 3), and gives evidence of having meaningful units as evidenced by appropriate reactions by the bees who witness the dances (as in 5). If the quality of the food source can be considered an abstraction, then these dances have the ability to refer to abstractions (as in 4). I haven't read about any scientific tests for innateness of these dances, although some researchers simply assume it. But, at the very least, creativity seems lacking. That is, although bees can indicate a range of location and quality, the parameters of what they can express are extremely limited. They cannot stray even slightly from these parameters. For example, they cannot convey that a new food source is near another well-known one. That is, they lack the ability to recombine the meaningful units of their dance in order to create novel ideas (as in 6), like we do when we play with morphemes to form new words and make use of some of the infinite possible ways of grouping words into constituents to form new sentences. Certainly communication takes place among bees, but are these three (or four) features of human language enough for us to call bee dances an instance of language as we understand that notion for humans?

Birdsong has also been extensively studied, and it is undisputed that birdsong transmits information. Messages such as

Here I am / Let's mate / There's a predator nearby / I found food / I found water / The nest is over here

have been observed and documented. Songs differ from species to species, and even within species songs can vary somewhat by the territory the bird occupies. That is, bird species can have song dialects. New Zealand saddleback males, when mating with a female from another territory (typically a widow), can adopt her dialect quickly (sometimes within ten minutes) and move into the new territory. So birds can learn dialects, and in fact they can learn a second song (analogous to a second language). They can even become polycantors (analogous to polyglots, those who speak many languages), mimicking the songs of other species and sometimes even nonbird sounds (e.g., noises of chainsaws or car alarms). It also appears that newly hatched birds immediately begin to acquire song, so they must be hard-wired for this task. Experiments with hand-raised, white-crown sparrows show that young males who do not hear adult males' songs within the first several months of life never develop a typical courtship-territorial song. Thus, it seems that birds have a critical period for acquiring song, just as humans have a critical period for acquiring language (see chapter 1).

The structure of songs also observes rules. For example, robins' song has several motifs that can be repeated in varying degrees, but these motifs must occur in a certain order or other birds will find the song unintelligible. At the same time, however, a fair amount of improvisation is observed, allowing the bird to express, perhaps, things like mood. In fact, when hens and turkeys and many other kinds of birds confront each other for the first time, they generally stop and face each other and make a variety of noises. Then they might attack, go in different directions, or feed side by side. Given this range of reactions, it seems that the birds are able to convey a variety of information and that the responses are not programmed but, instead, appropriate to the message.

To what extent then, is birdsong similar to human language? It appears to follow rules, to be innate, and to have meaningful units that result in appropriate responsive behavior. It doesn't seem to have displacement, as birds don't have songs about predators that passed by yesterday; they are able to refer only to those that are present. Songs can refer to abstractions in a limited way (danger or happiness). As with bees, it's clear that birdsong can convey many things. The parameters of that information are not so obvious with birds as they are with bees. Still, it does not appear that birds can tell each other about what just happened to them on the other side of the barn, for example. They simply don't have the necessary linguistic creativity to do so. Again, their communication system doesn't allow recombination of meaningful units in an infinite number of ways.

One might argue that birdsong is language of the type used by humans based purely on the claim that birds can learn human language—so they must have the capacity for language. Such a claim might be made after reading about Alex, an African gray parrot that Dr. Irene Pepperberg of the University of Brandeis worked with. Alex had an extensive vocabulary, supposedly comparable to that of a four- or five-year-old child. He could identify objects verbally, with English words, by their material, color, shape, and number. He could distinguish between objects according to any of these criteria. He knew the names of certain foods, such as *nut*, and he asked for them even when they were not present, exhibiting displacement. He used words that express emotions correctly and even apologized when he misbehaved, exhibiting the ability to refer to abstractions. So did he have language? He certainly learned to manipulate vocal tokens to give and get desired responses, and this facility would be explained if birds had a brain mechanism similar to the human language mechanism. Nevertheless, Dr. Pepperberg maintains that Alex did not talk as humans do. His verbal behavior was erratic, and she does not claim that he had language.

The sea mammals most studied with regard to language are whales and dolphins. During mating season, male humpback whales sing a complex song consisting of up to ten melodic themes, which are sometimes repeated all day long. All male humpbacks in the Atlantic Ocean sing the same song, and all male humpbacks in the Pacific Ocean sing the same song, but the songs of these two groups are different. No one is sure what the purpose of the song is because the whales do not seem to react to it and because, as I said, the song can go on all day long. Blue whales sing one kind of song when they are feeding and the males sing another during mating season, presumably to indicate reproductive fitness. This is the extent to which whale behavior exhibits anything like language as far as researchers now know. It has structure and it appears to be innate. Whether it displays evidence of meaningful units that are met with appropriate responses depends on whether you think noises made when eating or when wanting to mate are reflexive. But there's no evidence of any of the other three criteria fundamental to language used by humans.

Each Atlantic bottlenose dolphin has a unique whistle, what scientists call a signature. In addition, dolphins use a warning whistle in times of danger to the pod, and each pod of killer whales (which are a type of dolphin, not whale) appears to have a distress call unique to the pod. So when one pod's distress call is recorded and played for another pod, the other pod reacts only with curiosity. This dolphin behavior, then, exhibits structure, appears to be innate, and demonstrates limited ability to refer to abstractions (danger). Whether it displays evidence of meaningful units that are met with appropriate responses depends on whether you think flight or defense reactions to danger of the type practiced by dolphins is reflexive. Regardless, at least two criteria fundamental to human language are absent from dolphin communication, including the one I have been stressing, namely the ability to create novel expressions.

Some scientists have tried to teach human language to dolphins, just as some have tried to do with birds. Hand gestures that signify objects (such as surfboards, balls, and people), directions (right, left, up, and down), and actions (fetch) are taught to the dolphins, and they are able to respond appropriately. Indeed, they can interpret new utterances correctly. So dolphins who were taught that the sequence of gestures person-surfboard-fetch means 'bring the surfboard to the person' were able to interpret surfboard-person-fetch as 'bring the person to the surfboard' without any trouble. Clearly, the dolphins in these experiments recognized structural language rules and exhibited appropriate responses to meaningful units. However, it is still unclear what this tells us about whether their own dolphin sounds constitute a language. Also, as with Alex the parrot, what these dolphins do is extremely limited in comparison with how humans manipulate language.

Primates—including chimpanzees, gorillas, bonobos, and others—are the object of much of the research activity on animal language. Chimpanzees have several types of calls, grunts, barks, pants, wails, laughs, squeaks, and hoots. They use them to alert others to the location of food sources, to announce a successful kill after a hunt, to express alarm at danger or something that strikes them as peculiar, to identify themselves (like the signature whistles of dolphins), and to express satisfaction or peacefulness. Their postures, facial expressions, and limb gestures, however, play a greater role in communication. Yet none of their methods of communication gives evidence of being able to refer to abstract ideas, and no studies have offered any version of a chimpanzee grammar.

On the other hand, some researchers argue that they have taught chimpanzees human language, just as Dr. Pepperberg taught the parrot Alex. However, sign language was used because chimps do not have the physiology that would allow them to produce human language sounds. A chimp named Washoe was immersed in American Sign Language (ASL) from the age of ten months at the Chimpanzee and Human Communication Institute. When she first saw a swan, she made the signs for water and for bird. Was she creating a compound word for swan—thus exhibiting a generative language capacity—or was she simply naming the two things she saw? When she was an adult, she was given a baby chimp named Loulis, whom she adopted as her son. The scientists did not use ASL around Loulis, but Washoe did, and by the time Loulis was five years old (in 1984), he was using 132 reliably identified ASL signs (and there is debate about whether he used others). Certainly, the fact that Loulis learned the signs from Washoe could be taken as evidence for an innate language capacity. On the other hand, maybe making the signs was simply a game of mimicry that mother and son played together, for Washoe typically responded to the scientists' use of signs with mimicry.

A female lowland gorilla named Koko was also taught ASL. She amassed a vocabulary of more than one thousand signs, the most of any nonhuman. Koko's use of ASL is among the best-known instances of language experiments with animals. Primary and secondary schools often have videos of Koko signing.

A male bonobo named Kanzi also learned some language but in a different way. His case is particularly interesting because, like the chimp Loulis, no one tried to teach him language. Instead, the scientists were trying to teach his mother to communicate through a keyboard that had dozens of lexigrams and geometrical designs that represented words. Kanzi picked up the ability to use the keyboard on his own, just from observation, as human children pick up language. Once the scientists recognized what was going on, they actively taught Kanzi, and he acquired an understanding of more than five hundred spoken English words and about two hundred lexigrams. He has shown that he understands rules of grammar, that he can use displacement, and that he can create new sentences. His use of the keyboard, combined with his appropriate behavioral responses to spoken English, certainly look as if he has acquired language, though much more limited language than that of a small child, which, by the age of three, has the ability to spontaneously produce any number of novel words and sentences. Again, the evidence suggests that bonobos have the capacity to acquire language, so perhaps they have a language mechanism in the brain, although there is no evidence that they have their own bonobo language.

Vervet monkeys have three different kinds of vocalization. One tells others to run upward, one to hide in the bushes, and one to watch out on the ground. Each seems to be oriented toward escape from major predators (you climb a tree when leopards come, you race into the bushes when eagles come, you look around the ground carefully for snakes). Meaningful units are clear, but the other five characteristics of human language are not attested.

In my opinion, none of these findings offers convincing evidence that animals use among themselves a natural language that is comparable to human language with respect to the six criteria listed earlier, although bird communication is surprisingly close to the model. Still, studies of animal language have been fewer than studies of human language, and recent studies often debunk false assumptions we've had about animals. For example, most kinds of felines are solitary animals as adults, with the exception of lions. We might expect, then, that if felines had language, lions would be the most likely ones to exhibit it. In fact, lions have long been known to use a range of sounds: grunts, moans, puffs, roars, growls, meows (among the cubs), rumbles, and hums. They use these sounds as calls to their young and vice versa, as warnings, threats, signs of pleasure, and so on. Often their vocalizations are accompanied by facial expressions, including orientation of the ears, wrinkling of the skin above the nose, widening of the eyes, and lifting of the top lip. In contrast, the solitary tiger has been believed to be nearly silent, making only an occasional cough or roar. However, it turns out that tigers roar much more frequently than previously believed, although their roars are very low in pitch, around eighteen hertz, which is below the frequency band audible to humans. Such a low roar can travel long distances through dense forests, so perhaps tigers are as likely as lions to have or not have language.

Undoubtedly, future studies will uncover other facts about animal communication, but unless they yield very different results from those of past studies, it would appear that animal communication is quite different from language among humans. If animals have the capacity for humanlike language, as in the case of the primates I have mentioned, they are not using it among themselves. The capacity for human speech is carried by a particular gene: the FoxP2. The FoxP2 protein structures of animals, including other primates, are distinct from those of humans, and it appears that those distinctions found in the human gene allow for a range of expression suited to needs that are particularly human. Animal communication, on the other hand, may well have complexities that are different from those of human language, suiting needs particular to the different types of animals.

Further Reading

Alex Foundation. http://www.alexfoundation.org/ (accessed May 3, 2009).

Anderson, S. 2004. *Doctor Dolittle's delusion: Animals and the uniqueness of human language.* New Haven: Yale University Press.

Armstrong, E. 1973. *A study of bird song.* New York: Dover.

Balda, R., I. Pepperberg, and A. Kamil, eds. 1998. *Animal cognition in nature: The convergence of psychology and biology in laboratory and field.* San Diego: Academic Press.

Bekoff, M., and D. Jamieson. 1996. *Readings in animal cognition.* Cambridge, Mass.: MIT Press.

Bertram, B. 1978. *Pride of lions*. New York: Scribner.

Brainard, M. S. and A. J. Doupe. 2000. Auditory feedback in learning and maintenance of vocal behavior. *Nature Reviews Neuroscience* 1 (1): 31–40.

Bright, M. 1984. *Animal language*. Ithaca, N.Y.: Cornell University Press.

Davies, G. 2001. Bird brains. http://www.pbs.org/lifeofbirds/brain (accessed May 3, 2009).

De Luce, J., and H. Wilder, eds. 1983. *Language in primates: Perspectives and implications*. New York: Springer.

Findlay, M. 1998. *Language and communication: A cross-cultural encyclopedia*. Denver: ABC-CLIO.

Frisch, K. von. 1971. *Bees: Their vision, chemical senses, and language*. Ithaca: Cornell University Press.

Gorilla Foundation. Gorilla intelligence and behavior. http://www.gorilla.org/world/ (accessed May 3, 2009).

Griffin, D. 1984. *Animal thinking*. Cambridge, Mass.: Harvard University Press.

Jellis, R. 1977. *Bird sounds and their meaning*. London: British Broadcasting Corporation.

Margoliash, D. 1983. Acoustic parameters underlying the response of song-specific neurons in the white-crowned sparrow, *Journal of Neuroscience* 3 (5): 1039–1057.

Marler, P. 1980. Birdsong and speech development: Could there be parallels? *American Scientist* 58: 669–73.

Morton, E., and J. Page. 1992. *Animal talk: Science and the voices of nature*. New York: Random House.

Pinker, S. 1994. *The language instinct: How the mind creates language*. New York: Morrow.

Rogers, L., and G. Kaplan. 2000. *Songs, roars, and rituals: Communication in birds, mammals, and other animals*. Cambridge, Mass.: Harvard University Press.

Savage-Rumbaugh, S. 1986. *Ape language: From conditioned response to symbol*. New York: Columbia University Press.

———, S. Shanker, and T. Taylor. 1998. *Apes, language, and the human mind*. New York: Oxford University Press.

Sebeok, T., ed. 1968. *Animal communication: Techniques of study and results of research.* Bloomington: Indiana University Press.

————. 1977. *How animals communicate.* Bloomington: Indiana University Press.

————, and R. Rosenthal, eds. 1981. *The clever Hans phenomenon: Communication with horses, whales, apes, and people.* New York: New York Academy of Sciences.

Seyfarth, R. M., D.L Cheney, and P. Marler. 1980. Monkey responses to three different alarm calls: evidence of predator classification and semantic communication, *Science* 210 (4471): 801–803.

Snowdon, C., and M. Hausberger, eds. 1997. *Social influences on vocal development.* New York: Cambridge University Press.

Keywords

animal communication
animals and language

7
Can computers learn language?

As I am revising this chapter in 2008, humans can interact verbally with computers in multiple ways. To take a simple example, when I dial the operator at my college and request the campus directory, a recorded voice asks me for the name of the person I'd like to speak to. When I say the name, the recording responds, "Did you say [the name]?" If I respond positively, the phone number of that person is automatically dialed for me. If I respond negatively, the recording apologizes, and a human operator comes on the line. Here a voice recognition program is at play. Such programs have been around for quite some time, and they are used in a variety of situations. One of my friends, who has cerebral palsy and is a quadriplegic, has a computer that has been programmed to recognize her voice and make written files of whatever she says. She's used this program for years to "type" with her voice. There's no doubt, then, that voice recognition by computers is possible.

Therefore, when we hear the common claim that computers can learn language, we might not be skeptical, although we should be. Learning a language is a complex process that involves more than voice recognition. When we ask whether or not computers can learn language, we're asking whether we will be able to have conversations with a computer that are indistinguishable from those with another person.

People have been asking that question and trying to devise computer programs that will allow a positive answer since as early as 1950, based on the work of Alan Turing, a British mathematician. Turing developed a kind of competition in which an interrogator (by keyboard) tried to figure out which of two respondents was a human and which was a computer. He predicted that a computer program would be judged "human" in such a competition within fifty years.

In the 1960s the program ELIZA was developed, which did little more than convert an input statement into a question. The result was that conversations with ELIZA were jokingly claimed to resemble conversations with a psychotherapist. Between then and now, other programs have been developed. Every time you use a search engine, you engage in a rudimentary kind of conversation with a computer.

If you'd like to try out some current attempts at computer-human conversations, there are at least two that might interest you. One is a.1.i.c.e. (http://www.alicebot.org). To any statement or question you input, a.1.i.c.e. responds with a preprogrammed statement or question from its database—and that database is impressively large. Nevertheless, one of my students in the spring of 2001 managed to stymie a.1.i.c.e. with the question "How much wood could a woodchuck chuck if a woodchuck could chuck wood?" Another possibility is Daisy (http://www.leedberg.com/glsoft), which is not preprogrammed at all. Rather, Daisy stores your input and manipulates it. So when you first talk with her, she seems to have no intelligence whatsoever (all she can do is repeat what you type in), but if you spend absurdly large amounts of time with her, she gradually comes to form relatively coherent responses.

Despite what seemed to be a reasonable prediction at the time, now more than fifty years after Turing made his claim we still have not come up with a program that allows a computer to participate like a human in a conversation. Will we ever be able to? At this point, the answer to that question is, of course, speculation. However, some guesses are more informed than others. To help you make an informed guess, let's analyze some sample conversations and ask whether computers could have produced them. Consider conversation 1:

A. Where are you going?
B. I am going to school.

In thinking about what went into this conversation, we can begin with the most obvious facts. The first is that someone produced utterance A. We know computers can produce language—whether preprogrammed (like a.l.i.c.e.) or not (like Daisy)—so utterance A could have been said by either a human or a computer.

Response B is based on interpreting utterance A. Again, we know computers can do this to a certain extent. That is, they can analyze sentences to some degree, recognizing verbs, *you* as the subject, and *where* as a location question word. They can then match that sentence with the same verb(s), an appropriate subject, and possible location responses—often those that begin with *to* (such as *to work, to the grocery*, and in this conversation *to school*). However, if you say the sentences aloud, you will find them stilted. Instead of response B, what would sound more natural? Probably this:

C. School.

That is, in casual conversation, we typically answer in fragments rather than whole sentences. And even if we were to answer in a whole sentence, we wouldn't say, "I am going" but rather the contracted form, "I'm going."

These kinds of discrepancies between ordinary and stilted language highlight the fact that spoken language and written language differ. Both forms change over time, but changes in written language usually lag behind changes in spoken language. You might object that response B would be acceptable in conversation if an authority figure had said A. That is, the person who produced response B might be using polite or formal language because of the situation. We exploit these discrepancies in language in our various types of conversation—using more formal styles of language with teachers, employers, and doctors, for example, and less formal ones with siblings, best buddies, and other people from our own age group and background. Computer programs that aim for naturalness must face these issues, which human speakers take for granted.

However, these matters do not interfere with comprehension, and if they were the only types of problems computer programs had to face, the outlook for natural computer-human conversations would be good. So let's look at other conversations that raise thornier problems. Consider conversation 2, which starts with this question:

D. What's up?

Now consider these possible responses (and don't worry about how the question in D would be written):

E. Not much.
F. Got an exam in the morning.
G. Party on Parrish Beach.
H. A preposition.
I. North, of course.
J. Google.

If you're a student, you might answer E, F, G, or a whole range of other possibilities. If you're taking a linguistics class, you could well answer H. If you're standing in front of a wall map, you might answer I. If you're reading the stock page, you could answer J.

In other words, utterances take place within a context. Although sometimes the context imposes only minimally on the response (as in the situation in which a student is asking another student whether anything special is going on), at other times it allows for only a small range of appropriate answers.

The sensitivity to context covers not just particular situations but also information about cultural habits and facts about nature, mathematics, history, and so on. In short, just about anything can form the relevant context for a conversation. For example:

K. We're getting married, Dad.
L. Honey, come on in here, and bring four champagne glasses.

The father is communicating his approval and joy in sentence L by drawing on our knowledge that drinking champagne is a celebratory act.

M. I vomited again this morning.
N. Oh, my god. When's it due?

In interpreting sentence N as an appropriate response to sentence M, we are relying on the fact that morning sickness is often an early sign of pregnancy.

O. He's trying to draw a map of hypothetical countries that requires more than four colors in order to allow every contiguous country to be a different color.
P. The fool.

To see sentence P as a sensible conclusion given sentence O, we're relying on the fact that it is mathematically impossible to need more than four colors to draw such a map. A computer program that aims for natural conversation must somehow be sensitive to context in all of these different ways. These are gigantic problems, and they won't go away because people move into different places, using their various senses to understand their surroundings. They learn by experiencing the world in a number of ways. The reservoir of their accumulated knowledge feeds their language interactions (see also the discussion of pragmatics in chapter 2). Computers, on the other hand, do not gain experiential knowledge that allows them to understand contexts like those in the preceding examples because they don't have senses or cognitive abilities.

We could easily make mobile computers for home and the office; robots are already here, of course. In addition, we could equip them with cameras, so that they have something comparable to vision; tape recorders, so that they have something comparable to hearing; sensors for heat and weight and a variety of other physical characteristics, so that they have something comparable to touch; sensors for various scents, so they have something comparable to smell; and sensors for sweetness, saltiness, acidity, and so forth, so that they have something comparable to taste. If we program in enough information, computers might be able to detect the commonest things that human senses detect. But what about the less common ones? What about the nuances, many of which we rely on in understanding our world?

Computers may very well learn. One famous example is the chess-playing computer Deep Blue, which can adapt to new strategies as a chess game progresses. Nonetheless, the ways in which computers learn will limit what they can learn. Deep Blue, for example, can search through millions of possible move sequences, but it is by no means clear whether the heuristics and strategies Deep Blue uses amount to understanding a chess position. It is fast but narrowly limited. Analogous limitations will affect any computer's ability to manipulate language.

You might object that problems involving context are not so much problems of language as problems of communication in general. Perhaps computers would fare better if we limited ourselves to purely linguistic matters. Consider the following examples:

Q. John ate the pie on the windowsill.

Certainly the pie was on the windowsill, but was John also? He might have been. Compare these sentences:

R. John ate his dinner in the restaurant.
S. John ate the candy in that cute little bag.

For sentence R, John was in the restaurant when he ate. For sentence S, John was not in the bag when he ate. A computer must be programmed to allow the prepositional phrase in all of these sentences to be analyzed as either modifying the noun that immediately precedes it (yielding the sense in which the noun was in that place but the eating did not occur there) or as modifying the verb (yielding the sense that the eating occurred in that place). How does the computer make such a choice when it doesn't know what a restaurant is and what a cute little bag is and when it has no knowledge of John's relative size to either of these places? Certainly we could feed the computer a database that notes which words co-occur with which structures since in the real world there are probabilities associated with situations (people are more likely to eat in restaurants than in bags). However, if our sentence were describing a situation with a low probability, the computer would assign the wrong structure even when a human might well understand the correct one from the context. Also, if the database does not happen to cover the relative probabilities of two structures for a given set of words (for example, if we were talking of eating candy with respect to closets), the computer would be at a loss. In that case, we could build in a default structure since it is likely that one structure occurs with more frequency than another in general. However, the chance of accuracy is only as good as the probability of that structure occurring in general.

It has been estimated that if we considered only sentences with twenty or fewer words in English, we'd have a database of approximately 10^{30} sentences, and many of them could be understood in multiple ways. Consider just this silly little sentence:

T. I saw her duck.

In example T, I might have seen an animal or an action, or I might be performing the gruesome action of sawing a duck. In some varieties of English, I could also have seen a bra strap (*duck* can have that meaning.) And sentence T has only four words. The task with longer sentences is daunting.

Moreover, think about these sentences:

U. Why's Virginia so mad?
V. My sister lost her book.

In response V the sister could have lost her own book or Virginia's book or even some third person's book, although to get this last sense we would probably need some preceding sentences or other context. Contrast sentence V to the possible answer W:

W. My sister lost her cool.

In contrast to sentence V, sentence W has only one interpretation for *her*—my sister. How does the computer recognize this fact?

Commands present additional types of problems. There's a considerable difference between asking a computer to follow a command such as:

X. Record "Law and Order" at 9 P.M. on Channel 10.

and the following command, which my students thought of:

Y. If there's a movie on tonight with Harrison Ford in it, then
record it. But if it's *American Graffiti*, then don't bother
because I already have a copy of that.

Whereas I'm optimistic about computers being able to follow command X someday, a command like Y is more difficult. Command X involves activating the "record" function on a DVR (digital video recorder) and selecting a particular channel at a particular time. It doesn't even ask the computer to scan a list of TV programs. That is, "Law and Order" will be the only program shown at 9 P.M. on Channel 10. However, command Y asks the computer to scan a list of TV programs, recognize which ones are movies, filter out the particular movie *American Graffiti*, determine whether Harrison Ford is an actor in the remaining movies, and then activate the "record" function on the DVR at all the appropriate times on all of the appropriate channels. These are Boolean tasks, and Web search engines perform them all the time. However, normally we feed search engines operators like *and* and *not* and key vocabulary items that the operators have scope over (that is, have in their domain). In an order like Y, we'd be asking the computer to work from ordinary sentences, extracting the operations and then properly associating them with the correct vocabulary items, a much harder task.

All of the issues discussed in this chapter will arise no matter what human language a computer is dealing with. The problems are compounded when we ask computers to deal with more than one language, as in computer translation programs (see chapter 3 for issues in translating). For these reasons, I seriously doubt that people will ever be able to have conversations with computers that are indistinguishable from those with humans. I want to leave you with one final conversation, in which I give you a question and a list of possible answers. I leave it to you to think about the difficulties these examples present for computers:

Question: Why won't you go into that room?
Answers: Spiders.
        Superstition.
        No shoes.
        No windows.
        No reason.
        I won't tell you.
        Guess.

Further Reading

Deep Blue. http://www.research.ibm.com/deepblue/meet/html/d.3.html (accessed May 3, 2009).

Harley, T. A. 2008. *The psychology of language: From data to theory*, 3rd ed. New York: Psychology Press.

IEEE International Workshop on Robot and Human Interactive Communication Proceedings. 2000. New York: Institute of Electrical and Electronics Engineers.

Jurafsky, D., and J. H. Martin. 2000. *Speech and language processing: An introduction to natural language processing, computational linguistics, and speech recognition*. Upper Saddle River, N.J.: Prentice Hall.

McCarthy, J. 2007. What is artificial intelligence? http://www-formal.stanford.edu/jmc/whatisai/whatisai.html (accessed May 3, 2009).

Meeden, L. Developmental robotics. http://www.cs.swarthmore.edu/program/research/meeden.html (accessed May 3, 2009).

Neural information processing systems. http://nips.djvuzone.org/index.html (accessed May 3, 2009).

Sixth International Conference on Neural Information Processing. 1999. *Minds and machines: Journal for artificial intelligence, philosophy, and cognitive science.* Norwell, Mass.: Kluwer Academic.

Smith, G. 1991. *Computers and human language.* New York: Oxford University Press.

Keywords

computational linguistics
computers and language

part II

Language in Society

8 Can one person's speech be better than another's?

Not all speakers of a given language speak the same. Speech variations abound on television. Maybe you've seen the movie or the play *My Fair Lady*, in which Henry Higgins believes that the Queen's English is the superior language of England (and perhaps of the world). So the question arises whether one person's speech can be better than another's, and this question is subsumed under the larger question of whether any language is intrinsically superior to another. While we focus on speech here, analogous issues arise for sign.

Before facing this issue, though, we need to think about another matter. Consider these utterances:

> Would you mind if I borrowed that cushion for a few moments?
> Could I have that pillow for a sec?
> Give me that, would you?

All of these utterances could be used to request a pillow.

Which one(s) would you use in addressing a stranger? If you use the first one, perhaps you sense that the stranger is quite different from you (such as a much older person or someone with more stature or authority). Perhaps you're trying to show that you're polite or refined or not a threat. Pay attention to the use of the word *cushion* instead of *pillow*. Pillows often belong behind our heads, typically in bed. If you wanted to avoid any hint of intimacy, you might choose to use the word *cushion* for what is clearly a pillow.

Consider the third sentence. It's harder for some people to imagine using this one with a stranger. When I help to renovate urban housing for poor people with a group called Chester Community Improvement Project and I am pounding in nails next to some guy and sweat is dripping off both our brows, I have no hesitation in using this style of sentence. With the informality of such a sentence, I'm implying or perhaps trying to bring about a sense of camaraderie.

Of course, it's easy to imagine a scene in which you could use the second sentence with a stranger.

Which one(s) would you use in addressing someone you know well? Again, it could be all three. However, now if you use the first one, you might be insulting the addressee. It's not hard to think of a scenario in which this sentence carries a nasty tone rather than a polite one. And you can easily describe scenarios for the second and third sentences.

The point is that we command different registers of language. We can use talk that is fancy or ordinary or extremely informal, and we can choose which register to use in which situations to get the desired effect. So we have lots of variation in our own speech in the ways we phrase things (syntax) and the words we use (lexicon or vocabulary).

Other variation in an individual's speech involves sound rules (phonology). Say the third sentence aloud several times, playing with different ways of saying it. Contrast *give me* to *gimme* and *would you* to *wudja*. When we say words in a sequence, sometimes we contract them, but even a single word can be said in multiple ways. Say the word *interesting* in several sentences, imagining scenarios that differ in formality. Probably your normal (or least marked) pronunciation has three syllables: "in-tres-ting." However, maybe it has four, and if it does, they are probably "in-er-es-ting." The pronunciation that is closest to the spelling ("in-ter-es-ting") is more formal and, as a result, is sometimes used for humor (as in "very in-ter-es-ting," with a noticeably foreign flair to the pronunciation of *very* or with a drawn-out "e" in *very*).

So you have plenty of variation in your own speech, no matter who you are, and the more different speech communities you belong to, the more variation you will have. With my mother's relatives, I will say, for example, "I hate lobsters anymore," whereas with other people I'm more likely to say, "I hate lobsters these days." This particular use of *anymore* is common to people from certain geographical areas (the North and South Midland, meaning the area from Philadelphia westward through southern Pennsylvania, northern West Virginia, Ohio, Indiana, and Illinois to the Mississippi River) but not to people from other places, who may not even understand what I mean. With my sister, I used to say, "Ain't nobody gonna tell me what to do," but I'd never say that to my mother or to other people unless I were trying to make a sociolinguistic point. This kind of talk signaled for us a camaraderie outside of the socioeconomic group my mother aspired to. In a speech to a convention of librarians recently, I said, "That had to change, for I, like you, do not lead a charmed life," but I'd probably never say that in conversation to anyone—it's speech talk. Also, think about the language you use in e-mail, and contrast it to your job-related writings, for example.

Although we cannot explicitly state the rules of our language, we do choose to use different ones in different contexts. We happily exploit variation, which we encounter in a wide range from simple differences in pronunciation and vocabulary to more marked ones that involve phrasing and sentence structure. When the differences are greater and more numerous, we tend to talk of dialects rather than just variations. Thus, the languages of upper- and lower-class Bostonians would probably be called variations of American English, whereas the languages of upper- and lower-class Londoners (Queen's English versus Cockney) would probably be called dialects of British English. When the dialects are so different as to be mutually incomprehensible and/or when they gain a cultural or political status, we tend to talk of separate languages (such as French versus Spanish).

There's one more point I want to make before we return to our original question. I often ask classes to play the game of "telephone" in the following way. We line up twenty-one chairs, and volunteers sit on them. Then I whisper in the middle person's ear perhaps something very simple such as "Come with me to the store." The middle person then whispers the phrase into the ears of the people on both sides, and the whisper chain goes on to each end of the line. Finally, the first and twenty-first persons say aloud what they heard.

Next we do the same experiment, but this time with a sentence that's a little trickier, perhaps something such as "Why choose white shoes for winter sports?" Then we do the experiment with a sentence in a language that the first whisperer (who is often not me at this point) speaks reasonably well and that might be familiar to some of the twenty-one people in the chairs—perhaps something such as "La lune, c'est magnifique" (a French sentence that means 'the moon is wonderful'). Finally, we do the experiment with a sentence whispered initially by a native speaker of a language that none of the twenty-one people speak.

Typically, the first and twenty-first persons do not come up with the same results. Furthermore, the distance between them seems greater with each successive experiment.

Part of the problem is in the listening. We don't all hear things the same way. When we haven't heard something clearly, we ask people to repeat what they said. However, sometimes we don't realize we haven't heard something clearly until our inappropriate response is corrected. At times the other person doesn't correct us, and the miscommunication remains, leading to various other difficulties.

Part of the problem in the experiment is in the repeating. You may say, "My economics class is a bore," and you begin the second word with the syllable "eek." I might repeat the sentence but use my pronunciation of the second word, which would begin with "ek." If you speak French well, you might say *magnifique* quite differently from me. In high school or college language classes, the teacher drilled the pronunciation of certain words over and over—but some people never mimicked to the teacher's satisfaction. A linguist told me a story about a little girl who introduced herself as "Litha." The man she was introducing herself to said, "Litha?" The child said, "No, Litha." The man said, "Litha?" The child said, "No, no. Litha. Li-tha." The man said, "Lisa?" The child smiled and said, "Right." Repetitions are not exact and lead to change.

Imperfections in hearing and repeating are two of the reasons that language must change over time. When the Romans marched into Gaul and into the Iberian Peninsula and northeastward into what is now Romania, they brought large populations who stayed and spoke a form of street Latin. Over time, however, the street Latin in Gaul developed into French; that in the Iberian Peninsula developed into Portuguese along the west and Spanish along the east and central portions; that in Romania developed into Romanian. Moreover, the street Latin spoken in the original community on the Italian Peninsula changed as well, developing into Italian.

Other factors (besides our imperfections in hearing and repeating sounds) can influence both the speed and the manner of language changes—but the fact is that living languages necessarily change. They always have and they always will.

Many political groups have tried to control language change. During the French Revolution, a controlling faction decided that a standard language would pave the way for unity. Parish priests, who were ordered to survey spoken language, found that many dialects were spoken in different geographic areas, and many of them were quite distinct from the dialect of Paris. Primary schools in every region of France were established with teachers proficient in the Parisian dialect. The effect of this educational reform was not significant until 1881, when state education became free and mandatory, and the standard dialect (that is, Parisian) took hold more firmly. Still, the geographic dialects continued, though weakened, and most important, the standard kept changing. Standard French today is different from the Parisian dialect of 1790. In addition, new varieties of French have formed as new subcultures have appeared. Social dialects persist and/or arise even when geographic dialects are squelched. Change is the rule in language, so variation will always be with us.

Now we can ask whether one person's speech can be better than another's. This is a serious question because our attitudes about language affect the way we treat speakers in personal, as well as business and professional, situations. In what follows I use the term "standard American English" (a term riddled with problems that will become more and more apparent as you read)—the variety that we hear in news reports on television and radio. It doesn't seem to be strongly associated with any particular area of the country, although those who aren't from the Midwest often call it Midwestern. This variety is also more frequently associated with the middle class than with the lower class, and it is more frequently associated with whites than with other races.

A few years ago one of my students recorded herself reading a passage by James Joyce both in standard American English pronunciation and in her Atlanta pronunciation (she is white and from Atlanta). She then asked strangers (adults of varying ages who lived in the town of Swarthmore, Pennsylvania) to listen to the two readings and answer a set of questions she had prepared. She did not tell the strangers that the recordings were made by a single person (nor that they were made by her). Without exception, the strangers judged the person who read the passage with standard English pronunciation as smarter and better educated, and most of them judged the person who read the passage with Atlanta pronunciation as nicer and more laid back. This was just a small, informal study, but its findings are consistent with those of larger studies.

Studies have shown that prejudice against certain varieties of speech can lead to discriminatory practices. For example, Professor John Baugh of Washington University directed a study of housing in which he used different English pronunciations when telephoning people who had advertised apartments for rent. In one call he would use standard American pronunciation (i.e., white); in another, African American; in another, Latino. (Baugh is African American, grew up in the middle class in Los Angeles, and had many Latino friends. He can sound African American, white, or Latino at will.) He said exactly the same words in every call, and he controlled for the order in which he made the calls (i.e., sometimes the Latino pronunciation would be used first, sometimes the African American, and sometimes the standard). He asked whether the apartments were still available. More were available when he used the standard pronunciation. Thus, it is essential that we examine carefully the question of "better" with regard to language variety.

When I knock on a door and my friend inside says, "Who's there?" I'm likely to answer, "It's me," but I don't say, "It's I" (or, even more unlikely for me, "It is I"). Do you? If you do, do you say that naturally, that is, not self-consciously? Or do you say it because you've been taught that that's the correct thing to say? If you do it naturally, your speech contains an archaism—a little fossil from the past. We all have little fossils. I say, "I'm different from you." Most people today would say, "I'm different than you." My use of *from* after *different* was typical in earlier generations, but it's not typical today. Some of us hold onto archaisms longer than others, and even the most linguistically innovative of us probably have some. So don't be embarrassed by your fossils: They're a fact of language.

However, if you say, "It's I," self-consciously because you've been taught that that's correct, what does "correct" mean in this situation? If that's what most people used to say but is not what most people say today, you're saying it's correct either because you revere the past (which many of us do) or because you believe that there's a rule of language that's being obeyed by "It's I" and being broken by "It's me."

I'm going to push the analysis of just this one contrast—"It's I" versus "It's me"—quite a distance because I believe that many relevant issues about how people view language will come out of the discussion. Consider the former reason for preferring "It's I," that of revering the past. Many people have this reason for using archaic speech patterns and for preferring that others use them. For some reason, language is treated in a unique way here. We certainly don't hold up the past as superior in other areas, for example, mathematics or physics. So why do some of us feel that changes in language are evidence of decay?

If it were true that the older way of saying something were better simply because it's older, your grandparents spoke better than your parents, and your great-grandparents spoke better than your grandparents, and so on. Did Chaucer speak a form of English superior to that spoken by Shakespeare? Shall we go further back than Chaucer for our model? There is no natural stopping point. We can go all the way to prehistoric times if we use "older" as the only standard for "better."

The latter reason—believing that "It's I" obeys a rule that "It's me" breaks—is more defensible, if it is indeed true. Defenders of the "It's I" school of speech argue that, with the verb *be*, the elements on both sides of it are grammatically equivalent—so they should naturally have the same case.

I've used a linguistic concept here: case. To understand it (or review it), look at these Hungarian sentences:

Megnézhetem a szobát?	May I see the room?
Van rádió a szobában?	Is there a radio in the room?
Hol a szoba?	Where's the room?

I have translated the sentences in a natural way rather than word by word. Can you pick out the word in each sentence that means 'room'? I hope you chose *szobát*, *szobában*, and *szoba*. These three forms can be thought of as variants of the same word. The difference in form is called case marking. Textbooks on Hungarian typically claim that a form like *szoba* is used when the word is the subject of the sentence, a form like *szobát* when the word is the direct object, and a form like *szobában* when the word conveys a certain kind of location (comparable to the object of the preposition *in* in English). So a word can have various forms—various cases—based on how it is used in a sentence.

English does not have different case forms for nouns (with the exception of genitive nouns, such as *boy's* in *the boy's book*). So in the English translations of the preceding Hungarian sentences, the word *room* is invariable. However, English does have different case forms for pronouns:

> I like tennis.
> That tennis racket is mine.
> Everyone likes me.

These three forms indicate the first-person singular: *I, mine,* and *me.* They distinguish subjects (*I*) from genitives (*mine*) from everything else (*me*).

Now let's return to "It's I." Must elements on either side of *be* be equivalent? In the following three sentences, different syntactic categories are on either side of *be* (here "NP" stands for "noun phrase"):

> Bill is tall.   NP be AP
> Bill is off his rocker.   NP be PP
> Bill is to die for.   NP be VP

Tall is an adjective (here, an adjective phrase (AP) that happens to consist of only the head adjective). *Off* is a preposition, and it's part of the prepositional phrase (PP) *off his rocker. To die for* is a verb phrase (VP). Thus, the two elements that flank *be* do not have to be equivalent in category.

Still, in the sentence "It's I," the elements that flank *be* are both pronouns (*It* and *I*), so maybe these elements are equivalent in this sentence. Let's test that claim by looking at agreement. Verbs agree with their subject in English, whether that subject precedes or follows them:

> John's nice.
> Is John nice?

However, *be* in our focus sentence agrees with the NP to its left (which happens to be a single word, filling the NP), not to its right:

It's I.
*It am I.

No one would say "It am I." Therefore, the NP to the right of *be* is not the subject of the sentence, which means that the NPs flanking *be* are not equivalent—*It* is the subject, but *I* is not.

Perhaps you think that the equivalence that matters here has to do with meaning, not with syntax. Let's pursue that: Do *It* and *I* have equivalent meaning in "It's I"? Notice that you can also say:

It's you.

In fact, the slot after *It's* can be filled by several different pronouns. *It* in these sentences is not meaningful; it is simply a placeholder, similar (though not equivalent) to the *it* in sentences about time and weather:

It's four o'clock.
It's hailing.

However, *I* is meaningful because it refers to a person (the speaker). Therefore, *It* and *I* are not equivalent in meaning in the sentence "It's I."

In sum, it's not clear that the elements on either side of *be* in the sentence "It's I" are equivalent in any linguistic way. We can conclude something even stronger. We noted that *It* in these sentences is the subject and that the pronoun following a form of *be* is not the subject. But the pronoun following *be* is also not a genitive. Given the pronoun case system of English discussed earlier, we expect the pronoun to take the third form (the "elsewhere" form), which is *me*, not *I*. In other words, our case system would lead us to claim that "It's me" is the grammatical sentence.

I am not saying "It's I" is ungrammatical. I want only to show that the issue may not be as clear-cut as you might have thought. Indeed, the conclusion I come to is that more than one case system is at play here. Those who say "It's me" are employing regular case rules. However, those who say "It's I" have a special case rule for certain sentences that contain *be*. The important point is that both sets of speakers have rules that determine what they say. Their speech is systematic; they are not speaking randomly.

That is the key issue of this whole chapter. When we consider variation in language, we must give up the idea of errors and accept the idea of patterns. Some people produce one pattern because they are following one set of rules; other people produce a different pattern because they are following a different set of rules. (For several different types of language variations in English, visit the websites of the West Virginia Dialect Project: http://www.as.wvu.edu/dialect.) From a linguistic perspective, asking whether one person's speech can be better than another's would amount to asking whether one system is better. But what standards do we have for evaluating systems? What standards do you, as a speaker of the language, employ when you judge varieties of speech? To answer that question, consider variation in your own speech. Do you consider some varieties better than others? And which ones? If you're like most people, you consider formal or polite speech to be better. However, that standard concerns behavior in society—behavior that may reveal or perhaps even determine one's position. We tend to think that the speech of those who hold cultural, economic, or other social power is better, but this has little to do with linguistic structure.

Now ask yourself what standards you are using to judge the speech of others. Such questions often boil down to your politics (who do you esteem?) or to your experience (what are you familiar with?) but not to your grammatical rules. Consider the common claim that some varieties of speech are lazy. Try to find a recording of English speech that you consider lazy. Now mimic it. Some people are good at mimicking the speech of others, but accurately mimicking the speech of anyone else (anyone at all) takes a good ear, good control over the parts of your body that produce speech, and mostly a grasp of the sound rules that are being used. So the speech you thought was lazy wasn't lazy at all. Rather, different rules are being employed in these varieties of speech. What makes each variety distinct from others is its inventory of rules.

Consider learning a foreign language. People who feel confident about their ability to speak and understand a foreign language in a classroom often visit a place where that language is spoken only to find that no one is speaking the classroom variety. One of the big differences is usually speed: Ordinary speech can be quite rapid. Again, some claim that fast speech is sloppy, but fast speech is notoriously hard to mimic. It is typically packed with sound rules, so it takes more experience with the language to master all of the rules and to be able to produce fast speech.

Among American speakers a common misconception is that British speech is superior to American English. Part of this belief follows from reverence of the past, already discussed. Part of it follows from the misperception that American upper-class speech is closer to British speech—so British speech is associated with high society and with politeness. In fact, the speech of the British has changed over time, just as the speech of the American colonialists changed over time. Therefore, modern British speech is not, in general, closer to older forms of English than American speech is. Pockets of conservative varieties of English occur both in the

British Isles and in the United States, but most varieties on either side of the Atlantic Ocean have changed considerably. Also, British society is stratified, just as American society is, and not all British speech is either upper class or polite.

Linguists claim that all varieties of a language—all dialects and all languages, for that matter—are equal linguistic citizens. Linguists have recognized that all languages are systematic in that they obey certain universal principles regarding the organization and interaction of sounds, the ways we build words and phrases and sentences, and how we code meaning. However, this doesn't mean that all language is esthetically equal. I can recognize a beautiful line in a poem or a story, as I'm sure you can (though we might not agree). However, that beautiful line might be in archaic English, formal contemporary English, ordinary contemporary English, very informal contemporary English, African American Atlanta English, Italian American Yonkers English, Philadelphia gay English, Chinese American Seattle English, or so many others. Within our different varieties of speech, we can speak in ways that affect people's hearts or resonate in their minds, or we can speak in ways that are unremarkable. These are personal (esthetic or political) choices.

In chapter 12, I outline some possible effects of the goal of the English-only movement (EOM) of minimizing language variations in the United States. However, even if English were declared the official language of the United States, variation would not be wiped out. What would be threatened would be the richness of the range of variation most speakers are exposed to. Once that exposure is lost, Americans might start thinking that English is a superior language simply because they would no longer hear other languages being spoken by people they know personally and respect. They might become severely provincial in their linguistic attitudes, and given the necessity of global respect these days, such provincialism could be dangerous.

The fact that variation in language is both unavoidable and sometimes the result of aesthetic and/or political choices does not mean that educational institutions should not insist that children master whatever variety of language has been deemed the standard—just for purely practical reasons. There's little doubt that linguistic prejudice is a reality. The adult who cannot speak and write the standard variety may encounter a range of difficulties from finding suitable employment to achieving social advancement.

At the same time, all of us—and educational institutions, in particular—should respect all varieties of language and show that respect in relevant ways. Look at one notorious controversy: In 1996 the school board in Oakland, California, declared Ebonics to be the official language of the district's African American students. Given funding regulations for bilingual education in that time and place, this decision had the effect of allowing the school district to use funds set aside for bilingual education to teach their African American children in Ebonics, as well as in the standard language.

The debate was particularly hot, I believe, because of the sociological issues involved. Many people thought that Ebonics should be kept out of the classroom purely because the dialect was associated with race. Some of these people were African Americans who did not want their children to be disadvantaged by linguistic prejudice; they were afraid that teaching in Ebonics would exaggerate racial linguistic prejudice rather than redress it. Many good books written about the Ebonics controversy for the general public look at the issue from a variety of perspectives (see the suggested readings). However, from a linguistic perspective, the issue is more a question of bilingual (or bidialectal) education than anything else. If you care about the Ebonics issue, I urge you to read chapter 12, keeping Ebonics in mind.

In sum, variation in language is something we all participate in, and, as a linguist and a writer, I believe it's something we should revel in. Language is not a monolith, nor can it be, nor should it be, given the complexity of culture and the fact that language is the fabric of culture. Some of us are more eloquent than others, and all of us have moments of greater or lesser eloquence. However, that range in eloquence is found in every language, every dialect, and every variety of speech.

Further Reading on Variation

Andersson, L. G., and P. Trudgill. 1990. *Bad language*. Cambridge: Blackwell.

Ash, S. 2003. A national survey of North American dialects. In D. Preston, ed., *Needed research in American dialects*. Durham, N.C.: American Dialect Society, Duke University Press.

Baron, D. 1994. *Guide to home language repair*. Champaign, Ill.: National Council of Teachers of English.

Baugh, J. 1999. *Out of the mouths of slaves*. Austin: University of Texas Press.

Biber, D., and E. Finegan. 1997. *Sociolinguistic perspectives on register*. New York: Oxford University Press.

Cameron, D. 1995. *Verbal hygiene*. London: Routledge.

Carver, C. 1989. *American regional dialects: A word geography*. Ann Arbor: University of Michigan Press.

Coulmas, F. 1998. *Handbook of sociolinguistics*. Cambridge: Blackwell.

Fasold, R. 1984. *The sociolinguistics of society*. New York: Blackwell.

Finegan, E. 1980. *Attitudes toward language usage*. New York: Teachers College Press.

Fishman, J. 1968. *Readings in the sociology of language*. Paris: Mouton.

Herman, L. H., and M. S. Herman. 1947. *Manual of American dialects for radio, stage, screen, and television*. New York: Ziff Davis.

Hock, H., and B. Joseph. 1996. *An introduction to historical and comparative linguistics*. Berlin: de Gruyter.

Labov, W. 1972. *The logic of nonstandard English in language and social context: Selected readings*. Comp. Pier Paolo Giglioli. Baltimore: Penguin.

———. 1972. *Sociolinguistic patterns*. Philadelphia: University of Pennsylvania Press.

———. 1987. How I got into linguistics, and what I got out of it. http://www.ling.upenn.edu/~labov/Papers/HowIgot.html (accessed May 3, 2009).

———. 1995. Can reading failure be reversed? A linguistic approach to the question. In V. Gadsden and D. Wagner, eds., *Literacy among African-American youth: Issues in learning, teaching, and schooling*, 39–68. Cresskill, N.J.: Hampton.

———, S. Ash, and C. Boberg, eds. 2005. *Atlas of North American English: Phonetics, phonology, and sound change*. Berlin: de Gruyter.

LeClerc, F., B. H. Schmitt, and L. Dube. 1994. Foreign branding and its effects on product perceptions and attitudes. *Journal of Marketing Research* 31 (May): 263–70.

Lippi-Green, R. 1997. *English with an accent*. New York: Routledge.

McCrum, R., W. Cran, and R. MacNeil. 1986. *The story of English*. New York: Viking Penguin.

Millward, C. M. 1989. *A biography of the English language*. Orlando: Holt, Rinehart, and Winston.

Milroy, J., and L. Milroy. 1991. *Authority in language*, 2nd ed. London: Routledge.

Moss, B., and K. Walters. 1993. Rethinking diversity: Axes of difference in the writing classroom. In L. Odell, ed., *Theory and practice in the teaching of writing: Rethinking the discipline*. Carbondale: Southern Illinois University Press.

Peyton, J., D. Ranard, and S. McGinnis, eds. 2001. *Heritage languages in America: Preserving a national resource.* Washington, D.C.: Center for Applied Linguistics and Delta Systems.

Romaine, S. 1994. *Language in society: An introduction to sociolinguistics.* New York: Oxford University Press.

Scherer, K., and H. Giles, eds. 1979. *Social markers in speech.* New York: Cambridge University Press.

Seligman, C. R., G. R. Tucker, and W. Lambert. 1972. The effects of speech style and other attributes on teachers' attitudes toward pupils. *Language and Society* 1: 131–42.

Simpson, J. 2005. *The Oxford dictionary of modern slang.* New York: Oxford University Press.

Telsur Project. Linguistics laboratory, University of Pennsylvania. http://www.ling.upenn.edu/phono_atlas/home.html (accessed May 3, 2009).

Trask, R. L. 1994. *Language change.* London: Routledge.

Trudgill, P., J. K. Chambers, and N. Schilling-Estes, eds. 2002. *The handbook of language variation and change.* Malden, Mass.: Blackwell.

Weinreich, U. [1953] 1968. *Languages in contact: Findings and problems.* The Hague: Mouton.

Wolfram, W. 1991. *Dialects and American English.* Englewood Cliffs, N.J.: Prentice Hall.

———, and N. Schilling-Estes. 1998. *American English: Dialects and variation.* Oxford: Blackwell.

Wolfram, W., and B. Ward, eds. 2006. *American voices: How dialects differ from coast to coast.* Oxford: Blackwell.

Further Reading on Ebonics

Adger, C. 1994. Enhancing the delivery of services to black special education students from nonstandard English backgrounds. Final report. University of Maryland, Institute for the Study of Exceptional Children and Youth. (Available through ERIC Document Reproduction Service [EDRS]. Document no. ED 370 377.)

Adger, C., D. Christian, and O. Taylor. 1999. *Making the connection: Language and academic achievement among African American students.* Washington, D.C.: Center for Applied Linguistics and Delta Systems.

Adger, C., W. Wolfram, and J. Detwyler. 1993. Language differences: A new approach for special educators. *Teaching Exceptional Children* 26(1): 44–47.

Adger, C., W. Wolfram, J. Detwyler, and B. Harry. 1993. Confronting dialect minority issues in special education: Reactive and proactive perspectives. In *Proceedings of the Third National Research Symposium on Limited English Proficient Student Issues: Focus on Middle and High School Issues* 2: 737–62. U.S. Department of Education, Office of Bilingual Education and Minority Languages Affairs. (Available through ERIC Document Reproduction Service. Document no. ED 356 673.)

Baratz, J. C., and R. W. Shuy, eds. 1969. Teaching black children to read. Available as reprints from the University of Michigan–Ann Arbor (313–761–4700).

Baugh, J. 2000. *Beyond Ebonics.* New York: Oxford University Press.

Christian, D. 1997. Vernacular dialects and standard American English in the classroom. ERIC Minibib. Washington, D.C.: ERIC Clearinghouse on Languages and Linguistics. (This minibibliography cites seven journal articles and eight documents related to dialect usage in the classroom. The documents can be accessed on microfiche at any institution with the ERIC collection, or they can be ordered directly from EDRS.)

Dillard, J. L. 1972. *Black English: Its history and use in the U.S.* New York: Random House.

Fasold, R. W. 1972. Tense marking in black English: A linguistic and social analysis. Available as reprints from the University of Michigan–Ann Arbor (313–761–4700).

Fasold, R. W., and R. W. Shuy, eds. 1970. *Teaching standard English in the inner city.* Washington, D.C.: Center for Applied Linguistics.

Green, L. 2002. African American English: A linguistic introduction.
     New York: Cambridge University Press.

Pullum, Geoffrey. 2007. Language that dare not speak its name. *Currents.*
     University of California, Santa Cruz. http://www.ucsc.edu/
     oncampus/currents/97–03–31/ebonics.htm (accessed December 2,
     2009).

Wiley, T. G. 1996. The case of African American language. In *Literacy
     and language diversity in the United States*, 125–32. Washington,
     D. C.: Center for Applied Linguistics and Delta Systems.

Wolfram, W. 1969. A sociolinguistic description of Detroit Negro speech.
     Available as reprints from the University of Michigan–Ann Arbor
     (313–761–4700).

———. 1990 (February). Incorporating dialect study into the language
     arts class. *ERIC Digest.* Available from the ERIC Clearinghouse
     on Languages and Linguistics, Center for Applied Linguistics,
     4646 40th Street NW, Washington, D.C. 20016–1859 (telephone
     202–362–0700).

———. 1994. Bidialectal literacy in the United States. In D. Spener,
     ed., *Adult biliteracy in the United States*, 71–88. Washington, D.C.:
     Center for Applied Linguistics and Delta Systems.

———, and C. Adger. 1993. *Handbook on language differences and speech
     and language pathology: Baltimore City public schools.* Washington,
     D.C.: Center for Applied Linguistics.

———, and D. Christian. 1999. Dialects in schools and communities.
     Mahwah, N.J.: Erlbaum.

Wolfram, W., and N. Clarke, eds. 1971. *Black-white speech relationships.*
     Washington, D.C.: Center for Applied Linguistics.

Keywords

AAVE
Ebonics
language change and variation
sociolinguistics

9 Why do dialects and creoles differ from standard language?

Misunderstandings of dialect diversity and creoles have led to common claims that some languages are deficient, revealing carelessness or even stupidity. Indeed, language discrimination is tolerated by people who would never tolerate discriminatory remarks based on race, ethnicity, gender, sexual orientation, or many other characteristics. The goal of this chapter is to foster an understanding of what dialects and creoles are so that such misconceptions can be erased. Along the way we will encounter an astonishing fact about creoles, one that has been pivotal in the understanding of the human mind.

In chapter 8, we saw that language changes over time. This is a hard-and-fast rule. Some language communities are highly innovative linguistically, and over several hundred years the changes in their language might be drastic; other language communities are linguistically conservative, and the changes might be minimal. Nonetheless, over time there will be changes in every language.

In chapter 8 we also noted two factors that contribute to bringing about language change: We do not all hear the same way, and we do not all repeat exactly what we've heard. However, many other factors can be relevant to language change. One of the most important is contact with other languages.

American society is quite fluid, and families and individuals often move from place to place. These moves have linguistic

effects on individuals, although they are usually minimal, particularly for adults. They do not have effects on the overall language
community that a person or family moves into.

For instance, my oldest daughter was born in Boston, but we
moved to Chapel Hill, North Carolina, when she was six weeks
old. When she was a year old, we moved to Washington, D.C., and
lived in Mount Pleasant, a racially and ethnically mixed neighborhood, where her best friends spoke Korean, the Spanish of
El Salvador, and African American English. She went to a public
nursery program for three-year-olds in which all of the other children but two were African American (one spoke German, one
Korean.) She then went to a public bilingual prekindergarten and
then a kindergarten in which all of the other children but one
were native speakers of Spanish. When she was six, we moved to
Ann Arbor, Michigan, and she went to a public elementary school.
Although classes were held in English, about half of the students
were children of foreign graduate students at the University of
Michigan. Her two best friends' native languages were Swedish
and Japanese. When she was thirteen, we moved to Swarthmore,
Pennsylvania, to a linguistically unremarkable school district. She
studied Spanish and Latin all through high school. She then went
to Durham, North Carolina, for college, where she studied Italian,
and then to Philadelphia, Pennsylvania, for medical school. She
then lived in Manhattan, Tucson, and Arcata (California) and is
now living in Missoula (Montana). During the first twenty-two
years of her life, she heard English at home but spent most of her
summers in various parts of Italy.

If you heard my daughter Elena speak, I doubt you could
guess the richness of her exposure to other languages and to multiple varieties of English. When we first came to Swarthmore, her
friends would correct her for saying *pop* instead of *soda*, and she

pronounced the word *egg* with the same vowel that starts the word *ate* in standard English—but that changed. Although she never picked up a Philadelphia pronunciation, she no longer has any traces of a Midwestern one. I would bet that someone trained in regional variations of American English would have a lot of trouble pegging her speech. All of her exposure has somehow leveled out a lot of regional characteristics that she might have had if she had grown up exclusively in Chapel Hill, Washington, D.C., or Ann Arbor.

That's true of many of us: The more places we've lived in for a considerable period, the more likely our language will be somewhat sanitized of regional characteristics. However, the important point is that, wherever Elena went, none of her friends picked up from her any linguistic characteristics of the language community she had recently moved from. That is, Elena did not influence Ann Arborites to speak with a Washington, D.C., accent, nor Swarthmoreans to speak with an Ann Arborite accent. Elena's story is typical; the language of isolated individuals does not tend to have effects on language communities.

If, on the other hand, 30,000 people from our neighborhood in Washington, D.C., had moved to Ann Arbor (a town of only 60,000 inhabitants at the time), and if they had stayed through a few generations, there might have been noticeable linguistic influences from the newcomers on the language of the Ann Arborites. Moreover, if 3,000 people from Ann Arbor had moved to Swarthmore (a town that has about 6,000 inhabitants, including 1,350 students at the local college), and if they had stayed through a few generations, there might have been some suspiciously Midwestern ways of saying things at the local schools.

Large migrations of people do happen, of course. Sometimes the migrating people are more populous than the indigenous people, and the language of the immigrants supplants that of the latter. That happened when the British colonized Australia: The indigenous languages of Australia were all but wiped out. (The most populous Aboriginal language community, which speaks Walpiri, has around two hundred speakers as of the writing of this book.) Of course, the English spoken in Australia has changed over time and diversified regionally, so Australians can tell whether someone comes from Perth, Melbourne, Darwin, and so on. Australian varieties of English are now quite distinct from British varieties (as well as American, Canadian, Indian, Nigerian, etc.). However, standard Australian English is quite mutually comprehensible with standard British English and standard American English—so we tend to call them all dialects rather than separate languages.

What's the difference between a dialect and a variety? From a linguistic point of view it might be the extent of the linguistic differences between the two ways of talking, in that two dialects have less in common than two varieties of a language. However, in common parlance, it's largely a sociological and political matter. If a group of people sees itself as distinct from another group (distinct in any number of ways, including culture, politics, race, sexual orientation, etc.), these people may prefer to talk about dialects rather than varieties of a language.

At any given moment in time, such as now, there is a set of dialects. As time goes on, though, these dialects might change enough so that they are no longer mutually comprehensible. At that point, they probably have different governments, and we would probably call them separate languages rather than dialects. English and German are examples. That is, Germanic tribes settled in England, and both the immigrants' language and the original Old German of the tribes left behind on the mainland changed—each in separate and independent ways, with the result that English and German today are not mutually comprehensible. The fact that they share a somewhat close ancestor (what we call Proto-Germanic) means that they are related languages that belong to the Germanic family (which also includes Dutch, Flemish, and the Scandinavian languages of Norwegian, Swedish, Icelandic, and Danish, as well as Afrikaans, descended from Dutch).

However, migrating people do not always wipe out or displace the indigenous languages. Sometimes the former coexist with the indigenous people in such a way that both languages continue to be spoken. If the migrating people are numerous enough and stay long enough, their language can have serious linguistic effects on the entire community's language to the point that the resulting language has a lot in common with both of the previous languages. That happened when the Normans marched into England in 1066 and stayed. Old English was a Germanic language; Norman was a French dialect (French is in the Romance family). Over many generations, the language of the Normans influenced every aspect of the structure of English, so that today English is a Germanic language that has been greatly influenced by French.

You can see the mixed heritage of English all through the vocabulary. English has the Germanic word *tooth* beside the Romance root *dent-* (in *dental*); the Germanic word *hound* beside the Romance root *can-* (in *canine*); and the Germanic word *laugh* beside the Romance root *rid-* (in *ridicule*). Can you see the pattern? In general, the short words are Germanic, and the roots that must be part of longer words (so-called *bound roots*) are Romance. The Germanic words tend to feel ordinary or crude or tough, whereas the words based on Romance roots tend to feel a little more special, refined, or delicate. That's true even when the Romance words are short. For instance, *calf* is a Germanic word, and it's used for the animal, but *veal* is a Romance word, and it's used for the meat of the animal—as though by using the Romance name, we can see the meat as somehow different from that little animal in the barnyard. Speakers feel this difference even in slang today. Compare the impact of Germanic *mother* to the Romance *mamma* in these two casual utterances by (unenlightened) young men, looking at passing women:

> Boy, is she a mother.
> Boy, is she a mamma.

Which term do you think these hypothetical young men would use for a woman they found really attractive? Which would they use for a woman they found totally unattractive? Do you see a distinction? Some people say that *mamma* is more likely for the woman they consider attractive, probably because the Normans were the rulers—with all of the riches and the things wealth buys at their disposal—so their speech became associated with the upper class and with good things in general.

However, a much more common situation is one in which a language community comes in contact with another to varying degrees but not nearly so extensively as with the Normans in England. In cases of relatively limited or brief language contact (perhaps a generation or two), the visiting language will have little effect on the indigenous language, and that effect will typically be limited to vocabulary. Languages are relatively quick to borrow vocabulary, slower to borrow pronunciation, and slowest to borrow rules of word formation and sentence structure. Thus, many dialects of Spanish in the south of Spain in particular have words of Arabic origin because of the invasions of the Moors, but their word formation and sentence structure are Spanish. Other examples of this sort of situation are easy to come by.

A very different situation can arise, however. Let's say that two groups of people have to communicate with each other because they must conduct business together. Let's also say that they do not have a language in common and their languages are quite distinct from each other. Finally, let's assume that one of the languages is spoken by people who have a lot of authority in this situation, whereas the other is not. For example, one language might be French, and the other might be a mix of the languages of African slaves—a situation that arose in Haiti. Or one language might be English, and the other might be a mix of the languages of Papua, New Guinea—another real situation. What do you think will happen?

What would you do if you were put into a room with someone who spoke Japanese, the two of you did not share a language, and the Japanese person had to work for you in getting a particular job done? (In other words, you are the one with the authority.) You'd probably resort to gestures and pointing but quickly discover that impromptu gestures have severe limitations in their communicative possibilities. Thus, you'd want to use language. You're the authority figure, so you'd probably prefer teaching the other person some English words for some of the tools you both are using rather than learning the Japanese words yourself. Perhaps you'd also name the pieces of the machine you're putting together and various other items you have to refer to, as well as a few actions, so that you're ready to work.

However, now that you've got some words in common, how do you put them together? There's a lot more to language than a set of words. Are you going to say, "Would you please pick up the second wrench on your left right away and tighten this bolt while I hold the chassis in place?" This sentence has too many words and too complex a structure for easy comprehensibility. Which words have meanings that you must absolutely convey? Perhaps these are *pick up, second, wrench, left, right away, tight,* and *bolt.* Perhaps you'll use *get* instead of *pick up,* for simplicity's sake. You may repeat *fast* rather than say *right away* for the same reason, and the whole idea of "while I hold the chassis in place" might not even be necessary. Therefore, you may try stringing together these key words: "Get second wrench, left, fast fast, tight bolt." It sounds dreadful but might be effective even though it is missing a lot of the connective "tissue" of language. On the other hand, it does have normal English word order.

If the Japanese person were to try to convey that same information to you, using the same words, she might say something like this: "Bolt tight, fast fast left second wrench get." Verbs come at the end of a sentence in Japanese.

The bare-bones contact language you and the Japanese person were creating is called a pidgin. Pidgins arise often and all over the world. The language of the authority figure is typically called the superstratum; the other language the substratum. The pidgin tends to have the vocabulary of the superstratum but the sentence structure of the substratum. Why? Generally, there isn't a one-to-one correlation between the set of employees and the set of employers. There might be a hundred people working for a single authority figure. You know, from the discussion of dialects, that language communities are quick to borrow vocabulary but slow to accept innovations in sentence structure. So the substratum, which typically has more speakers, determines the sentence structure of the pidgin. Still, individual speakers of a pidgin might employ their own private methods for putting sentences together. In fact, both the pronunciation and the sentence structure are highly unstable from speaker to speaker.

Here's a real sentence from a Japanese-English pidgin (taken in April 2000 from the following website, which is no longer extant: http://grove.afl.edu/~jodibray/LIN3010/Study_Aids/pidgin.htm):

> da pua pipl awl poteto it.
> the poor people only potatoes eat
> "The poor people ate only potatoes."

Here's another real sentence from a Filipino English pidgin (from the same website):

> wok had dis pipl.
> work hard these people
> "These people work hard."

As you might guess, the verb comes in the beginning of the sentence of the substratum Filipino language (Tagalog).

Pidgins are special languages in that they have no native speakers. All those who speak a pidgin also speak their native language.

Pidgins often come into existence when the right kind of contact situation arises and then cease to exist when that situation dissipates, but sometimes the situation prevails for a long time. In that case, children are born into the pidgin-speaking community. They are exposed to the pidgin from the beginning, making their linguistic situation unique.

One of the most marvelous facts discovered by linguists is that the very first generation of children born into a pidgin-speaking community develops its own language, called a *creole*, which has vocabulary in common with the pidgin but a set of rules for sentence formation that is not derived from either the superstratum or the substratum. The rules that creoles exhibit are found in many languages that are not creoles—they are natural rules of language. However, the most amazing fact of all is that creoles around the world, regardless of their superstratum and substratum, have much in common with each other. There are more than one hundred creoles in the world, so their common characteristics cannot simply be accidental. Before the technological advances that allowed for brain imaging and other kinds of experimental work, and before the discovery of the gene FoxP2, the structure of creoles was one of the strongest pieces of evidence for the existence of a language mechanism in the brain.

Typical characteristics of creoles include the following:

1. Creoles tend to have simplified vowel systems, often with only five vowels. In contrast, standard American English (for a discussion of the notion of "standard," read chapter 8), for example, has twelve vowels. This claim might surprise you since we identify only five letters of the Roman alphabet as vowels, but English distinguishes twelve vowel sounds. Say these words:

bat, bet, bait, bit, beat

There are five different vowel sounds here (and two of them might well be lengthened in a particular way, when it is then called a diphthong). Now say these words:

cod, cawed (as in the sound of a crow), code, could, cooed
    (as in the sound of a dove)

There are five vowel sounds here (again, two of them might well be lengthened in some varieties of English), and they are distinct from the vowel sounds in the first list of words. Now say these two words:

but, gallop

The vowel sound in *but* and that in the second syllable of *gallop* are probably distinct from any of the vowel sounds in the other two word lists—which is what I mean when I say that American English has twelve vowels.

The five vowels that many creoles have are typically (similar to) those found in these English words:

cod, bait, beat, code, cooed

2. Creoles tend to have a relatively restricted vocabulary, although it is much more extensive than that of pidgins. Nevertheless, words are used for a range of meanings in a creole, and everything people need to express is expressible, just as it is in any other natural human language. Notice that any language uses the same words for many meanings. Compare the (partial) range of the senses of *run*:

I run to the store.
Those stockings run too easily.
You can't run such a complicated business.
We run ourselves crazy with too much to do.
Rivers run downhill.
Children's noses run in the winter.
But our cars never run in the winter.

Just for fun, make your own list of the (partial) range of the meanings of *give*.

3. Creoles tend to express variations in time by having a string of helping verbs rather than by having complicated word-formation rules. In other words, they are more like English in this respect than like a language such as Italian:

English: I thought she might have been sleeping.
Italian: Pensavo che dormisse.

The idea of potential (in the English *might*), completed, or whole action (in the English *have*), and stretched-out activity (in the

English *been*) that go with *sleeping* are all expressed in the ending on the Italian verb *dormisse*. (*Dorm-* is the root for 'sleep'; *-isse* is the ending that carries all of the meaning about the time frame.) Here's an example from Hawaiian Creole English (taken in April 2000 from the following website, which is no longer extant: www.ac.wwu.edu/~sngynan/sbc3.html):

> George been stay go play.
> "George might have been playing."

4. Creoles tend to express negation by placing a negative word immediately in front of the first verb, whether it is a main verb or an auxiliary (as opposed to English, which expresses negation by placing the negative (usually a form of *not*) after the first auxiliary verb). The following example is from Raro-tongan, a Maori English creole, spoken on one of the Cook Islands:

> Jou no kamu ruki me.
> you—not—have—look—me
> "You have not seen me."

5. Creoles tend to place the verb between the subject and the object (as English does) and as in the preceding example from Rarotongan).

Creoles are spoken all over the world. The superstrata of most creoles are European languages, although the superstrata of certain creoles are an American Indian language (Chinook, Delaware, or Mobilian), Arabic, Malay, Swahili, Zulu, and so on. Because of the way in which creoles originate, they are often considered substandard languages, although linguistically there is nothing substandard about them. The creole Tok Pisin has in fact become the official national language of Papua, New Guinea.

The situations in which languages come in contact with each other vary enormously, and the effects of language contact vary accordingly. Language contact is undoubtedly one of the most important factors in language change, one that can bring about striking and radical changes, sometimes in a short period of time (as with creoles). Just as undoubtedly, change will occur even when a language is isolated from other languages.

Further Reading

Appel, R., and P. Muysken. 1987. *Language contact and bilingualism.* London: Arnold.

Arends, J., P. Muysken, and N. Smith, eds. 1995. *Pidgins and creoles: An introduction.* Amsterdam: Benjamins.

Bickerton, D. 1981. *Roots of language.* Ann Arbor: Karoma.

Cable, G. W. [1884] 1970. *The creoles of Louisiana.* New York: Scribner's

Görlach, M. 1991. *Englishes: Studies in varieties of English 1984–1988.* Amsterdam: Benjamins.

Gynan, S. Pidgins and creoles. http://www.ac.wwu.edu/~sngynan/slx3. html (accessed May 3, 2009).

Hartman, J. 1998. Words & stuff: cc: pidgin carriers. http://www.kith.org/ logos/words/upper2/CCreole.html (accessed May 3, 2009).

Holm, J. 1988–1989. *Pidgins and creoles,* 2 vol. Cambridge: Cambridge University Press.

———. 2000. An introduction to pidgins and creoles. Cambridge: Cambridge University Press.

Krelerak/Creoles. Available at: http://www.geocities.com/Athens/9479/ kreole.html (accessed May 3, 2009).

Myers-Scotton, C. 1993. *Social motivations for codeswitching: Evidence from Africa.* Oxford: Clarendon.

Numbers in pidgins, creoles, and constructed languages. http://www. zompist.com/last.htm (accessed May 3, 2009).

Post-contact languages of western Australia. http://coombs.anu.edu.au/ WWWVLPages/AborigPages/LANG/WA/4_7.htm (accessed May 3, 2009).

Romaine, S. 1988. *Pidgin and creole languages*. New York: Longman.

———. 1989. *Bilingualism*. Oxford: Blackwell.

———. 1994. *Language in society*. New York: Oxford University Press.

Sebba, M. 1997. *Contact languages: Pidgins and creoles*. New York: St. Martin's.

Thomason, S., and T. Kaufmann. 1988. *Language contact, creolization, and genetic linguistics*. Berkeley: University of California Press.

Todd, L. 1990. *Pidgins and creoles*. London: Routledge.

Weinreich, U. 1953. *Languages in contact: Findings and problems*, 2nd ed. The Hague: Mouton.

Winford, D. 2003. *An introduction to contact linguistics (Language in society)*. Malden, Mass.: Blackwell.

Keywords

creoles
dialect versus language
language contact
pidgins

10 Do men and women talk differently? And who cares?

In earlier chapters, I discussed three important factors that influence language change: the fact that people don't all hear the same (chapter 8), the fact that people don't all repeat in the same way (also chapter 8), and contact among different languages (chapter 9). However, even if there were a linguistic community in which people actually did all hear and repeat language in the same way and even if that community were monolingual and totally isolated from other linguistic communities, its language would change over time because other factors influence language change, factors internal to a society. In this chapter we look at the interaction of gender roles and language, but first let's briefly consider a larger question.

Why do social factors bring about language change? There are many theories, but they tend to boil down to one basic concept. Imagine that we live in a society in which everyone dresses the same. How long do you think this will continue? Not too long— someone is going to shorten a hem, roll up a T-shirt sleeve (perhaps carrying a little pad of Post-its in the newly created pocket), use a shawl as a festive skirt, or keep wearing jeans long after the threadbare stage. Even if most of us ignore the change, some might copy it, and sometimes most of us will copy it. If enough of us do so, of course, it's no longer a daring thing to do. It becomes the new status quo, and then we wait for another iconoclast.

139

People experiment with language and thus bring about language change, just as they experiment with hemlines and bring about style change. The interesting difference, however, is that language does not change in arbitrary ways but rather in ways that conform to general principles. As native speakers of our language, we do not have a conscious and explicit knowledge of these principles, just as we don't have an explicit knowledge of the process of the metabolism of sugar (except for the chemists among us). Nevertheless, we adhere to those principles, and if our pancreas is healthy, we metabolize sugar.

What are these principles? Let me give a small example. Several years ago, it was popular among young people to say a sentence and then put a negative at the end, a kind of sarcasm. For example, if you had asked your teenage son what he was going to do after dinner on a Friday night, he might have said, "I'm going to be studying for hours...not." This usage was widespread, and I wondered at a certain point whether it might actually become part of American English sentence structure. Putting a marker (like *not*) at the beginning or end of an utterance that the marker relates to (or, as linguists and philosophers would say, "operates over") is common in language. Some Chinese questions can be structurally identical to statements, for example, the only difference being the presence of a question marker (*ma*) at the end. Thus, the English negative structure was not in violation of any general linguistic principles. It did not, in fact, last long, but the point is that it could have.

On the other hand, if someone had ever tried to introduce a negative structure such as "I am not going not not to be not not not studying not not not not for hours," it would never have had a chance of catching on. What I did here was to add after the verb form the number of *nots* that corresponded to its position in the sentence. So the first verb form, *am*, had one *not* after it. The second, *going*, had two, and so on. Why is this structure so strange from a linguistic point of view? It seems that language principles do not allow counting linguistic units beyond three at most, whether in the sound system, the word-formation system, the sentence-structure system, or the meaning system. We are hard-wired not to do it. (Most of the chapters in part I should convince you that it makes sense to talk about being hard-wired for language.)

Let's return to our linguistically isolated and homogeneously monolingual community. Someone introduces a language change that adheres to general linguistic principles. Which potential changes actually endure and become the new status quo? It is impossible to predict. Languages often look as if they are heading in a certain linguistic direction and then change course. No reputable linguist will predict language change.

Still, we know that certain factors are important in language change within a linguistic community: race, ethnicity, social class, educational background, age, and gender, among others. Much has been written about these factors (and others), but that material is usually aimed at linguistic scholars. An exception is gender: Quite a lot has been written for the general public about the male and female use of language, particularly conversational behavior. The question of whether men and women talk differently is at least as important to the general public as any other question about gender roles, and it is arguably more important because language is such an intrinsic part of our identities.

The first step in answering that question is simply to collect data, but unless the data collection is designed to test specific hypotheses, the crucial evidence that would distinguish between competing hypotheses is often missing, so varying conclusions can be consistent with a single set of data. Furthermore, sometimes

data collection is not done in a scientific manner but rather anec-
dotally. Anecdotes may, in fact, reveal important truths, but to
be convinced of that, we need wide-ranging data that have been
collected with the most scrupulously scientific methodology. We
should keep this in mind as we proceed.

Some scholars have claimed that women and men in the
United States talk differently in several ways. Let's consider six
common and representative claims that I have come across in the
literature:

1. Men interrupt women more than vice versa.
2. Men ignore the topics that women initiate in conversation.
3. Men do not give verbal recognition of the contributions
   women make to conversation.
4. Men use more curse words and coarse language than women,
   whereas women use more apologies, hedges (devices to
   mitigate assertions, such as *I'm not an expert, but...*) and
   indirect requests.
5. Men use more nonstandard forms (such as *ain't*) than
   women.
6. Men are more innovative, accepting language change more
   readily than women.

Students are often familiar with claims 1 through 4—or, if not
familiar, tend to find them probable—but they may never have
thought about the other claims and have no idea of whether or
not they are probable. Claims 1 through 4 concern conversational
behavior that the ordinary person is sensitized to. Many of us were
taught as children that some of the behavior attributed to males in
claims 1 through 4 is rude and shouldn't be done. Claims 5 and 6,
on the other hand, concern conversational behavior that linguists
are more likely to notice than the ordinary public. I include them

because they are among the most important for anyone who cares about language change.

Consider the first three claims. How do they differ from the next three? That is, what aspects of language are the first three claims about, and what aspects of language are the second three claims about? The first three involve interactive behavior in a conversation, whereas the last three involve individuals' speech patterns.

Try to imagine a conversation with someone who (1) interrupted you, (2) did not pay attention to the topics you introduced, and (3) did not acknowledge your contributions to the conversation. Have you ever been in such conversations? Why did you stay in the conversation, if in fact you did? You may have stayed because the other person was an authority figure, perhaps your boss, your doctor, or your teacher. In that case, your leaving might have had adverse consequences for you.

Indeed, the first claim has been shown to be wrong in at least one study. Further, the first three claims about men's versus women's language have been challenged on the grounds that, in single-sex conversations, if one person has more power than the other person, these same characteristics of conversational behavior are found. In other words, the first three claims are, according to some scholars, really about power differences, not about sex differences—an example of why data collection needs to take into account a range of possible (and sensible) hypotheses. If your data on conversational behavior involve only mixed-sex conversations, you cannot know whether the characteristics you find follow from the sex differences or from other possible differences in the conversation partners—other possible differences might manifest themselves in somewhat complex ways.

Here's an example of real conversation (recorded by one of my students in a class on oral and written language in the fall of 2001). The two speakers are discussing a novel:

N: It was funny.
T: It was really descriptive.
N: It was funny how um the cat switched bowls. He uh fell into the bowl and breathed in the milk into his ear. It was...
T: I liked that one.
N: Yeah.

As you can see, T interrupted N and also ignored the topic of humor until N repeated and elaborated on it. These two speakers are middle-school boys. They are the same age, and the conversation is taking place at T's house, which might give T an advantage; on the other hand, N is the guest, which might give him an advantage. According to claims 1–3, T exhibits more male conversational behavior than N does, but even in this snippet of conversation we can recognize that the language interaction is complex. When T ignored what N said about humor, N ignored what T said about descriptiveness. They both wanted to put forth their ideas but were ready to acknowledge the other when forced. Is this typical of same-sex conversations?

Here's another example (recorded by another student in that class):

J: Um, how was your camp?
S: It was good.
J: What did you do?
S: Um, lots of stuff. I did a basketball clinic. That was fun.
J: Yeah. Um.

S: What was your favorite part?

J: Um, I think everything was my favorite part.

S: What was your specific...

J: Did you do a lot of crafts?

S: Not too many. I made a mask.

As you can tell, J interrupts S and ignores S's unfinished but predictable question. These two speakers are sisters; J is nine and S is fifteen. According to claims 1–3, J exhibits more male conversational behavior than S does. Given the age difference, we might be surprised that J seems to behave like the more powerful of the two, but if you consider the dynamics of the conversation, S seems solicitous of J—just as a big sister might be when a six-year gap is involved. It is important to notice that this same-sex conversation is quite distinct in participant interaction from the preceding one.

These are just two examples, although my classes over the years have collected hundreds. Almost all of them present interesting complications for claims 1–3, suggesting that factors beyond gender are relevant—perhaps age, familial relationships, location of the conversation, and so on.

The last three claims, although about individuals' language, still present tricky questions for the researcher. Consider number 4: Do the social relationships of the two members of a conversation affect the degree to which they curse? For example, if they are teenage siblings, the girl is older than the boy, and there is cursing, does the male still curse more than the female? Not in some of the conversations I've witnessed. If there's one adult male with three adult females in an office, one of the females is the boss of all the other people, and there is cursing, does the male still curse more than any of the females?

Even if we disregard the societal relationships of the people and consider only gender, some questions still arise: Are women more likely to curse with other women than with men? Are men more likely to curse with other men than with women?

As far as I can tell, claims 4 and 5 are well documented, but exactly what they tell us about men versus women is unclear. The prevalence of coarse language among men and hedges, apologies, and indirect requests among women (claim 4) is surely not evidence of any structural difference between the ways in which men and women talk or of any difference in brain structure between the two sexes. Rather, this difference most probably follows from conventions about the levels of politeness that men and women are expected to maintain in conversation. In other words, the difference is sociological and culture bound, not physiological. The prevalence of nonstandard forms among men (claim 5) is also probably a purely sociological fact in that nonstandard forms are more likely to be taken as less refined; women in our society are traditionally expected to speak in a more refined manner than men.

On the other hand, claim 6 is simply wrong. Women often apply new sound rules of certain types more aggressively than men, whereas men are more aggressive in applying new sound rules of other types. It appears that women's speech has a greater orientation toward prestige norms than men's speech does. In other words, women, more readily than men, adopt innovations that are considered to be high class or smart, using language to try to get ahead economically and socially.

All six claims, then, are more about sociological factors than linguistic ones. It is an important fact, for example, that we do not find generalizations such as the following: Women always use certain tenses on verbs, have a different set of word stress rules than men, or always place a preposition as the second word of their utterances. These are hypothetical examples of the types of differences that could conceivably develop if men and women really had different linguistic systems—but such hypotheticals never do come up in English. The grammar (i.e., the linguistic description) of women's speech in English is identical, as far as I know, to that of men's speech.

This is not to say that we don't associate certain grammatical patterns with gender, but gender roles are not the same as one's sex. For example, consider vocabulary use. *Lovely* or *divine* might be seen as words belonging to feminine language. A more feminine man might easily use these words, however, whereas a more masculine woman might not. So, again, these differences are related to societal roles, not to sex. We cannot claim that the grammar of women's speech is different from that of men's.

The preceding example of vocabulary choice relates to the United States. In various other countries, examples of differences between what men and women say can come from other parts of the grammar, as well as from the lexicon. Japanese, for example, has a number of first-person pronouns, some of which are generally used by women, some generally by men, and some by either. However, gay women have reported choosing to avoid the so-called feminine pronouns (such as *atashi*) in favor of the masculine pronouns (such as *boku*). Likewise, women tend to use certain sentence-final particles, but gay men may choose to use them as well. So, again, the linguistic differences are ones of sociological gender roles, not physiological sex.

The question of whether physiological sex is ever the true factor in speech differences between men and women needs to be approached carefully. It is impossible to learn whether sex or sociological role is the distinctive characteristic for a certain linguistic usage in societies that do not tolerate overt gender role crossing and in which the power of men over women is stable regardless of the situation. Therefore, the place to look is in other societies, like that of the United States, in which gender role crossing is tolerated and/or in which men can have power over women and vice versa, depending on the situation.

If you'd want to undertake a systematic study of a particular language phenomenon with an eye toward whether physiological sex, gender roles, or power relationships are pertinent in its analysis, you'd have to control for as many of the potentially relevant factors as you could. For example, let's say that you observe a situation in which a man and a woman exhibit distinct linguistic behavior regarding the use of a given word X. Let's also say that the man in the situation was traditionally masculine and the woman was traditionally feminine. I'm going to call this pair A. You can then search for other instances of that (type of) situation, in which you find the following:

B. two traditionally masculine men
C. two traditionally feminine women
D. a feminine man and a traditionally masculine man
E. a feminine man and a traditionally feminine woman
F. two feminine men
G. a feminine man and a masculine woman
H. two masculine women

By varying the people in this manner, you might be able to tease apart the influence of physiological effect (if any) from gender roles (if any). However, you can be sure of your results only if you control for power relationships, so for each type of pair you will have to find situations like these:

A.' Both people have equal power over each other.
B.' One person has more power over the other.

Furthermore, you'll have to test for a variety of ways in which people can have unequal power, including differences in age, education, finances, authority, and race. You will even have to consider matters as ordinary as whether the conversation is taking place in a neutral environment or one in which one of the speakers feels more comfortable than the other.

It's a daunting business and unavoidably so. Because sociological factors are many and varied, sociolinguistic studies have to use impeccable methodology if they are to have a chance of getting reliable results (results that can be duplicated or confirmed in other studies). Most sociolinguistic studies, for that reason, utilize a large sampling of people and present data that can be tested for statistically significant similarities or differences on a wide range of sociological factors.

The introduction to this book promises to help you recognize how to use your own knowledge of language to answer many of the common questions people have about language, but here I hope I have impressed on you the need for serious study before making generalizations. These two positions are not contradictory. If you know how to approach language data, you can recognize factors relevant to the issue at hand and see the sorts of questions that must be answered before conclusions can be considered reliable. In the case of language and gender issues, these questions are far too many and complex to be ignored.

Further Readings

Coates, J. 1993. *Women, men, and language*. New York: Longman.
Coates, J. ed. 1998. *Language and gender: A reader*. Oxford; Blackwell.

————, and D. Cameron, eds. 1989. *Women in their speech communities*. New York: Longman.

DeFrancisco, V. 1991. The sounds of silence: How men silence women in marital relations, Discourse and Society 2(4): 413–423.

Eckert, P. 1989. The whole woman: Sex and gender differences in variation. *Language Variation and Change* 1: 245–67.

Hall, K., and M. Bucholtz, eds. 1995. *Gender articulated: Language and the socially constructed self*. New York: Routledge.

Labov, W. 1990. The intersection of sex and social class in the course of linguistic change. *Language Variation and Change* 2: 205–54.

Lakoff, R. 1990. *Talking power: The politics of language in our lives*. New York: Basic Books.

McCay, S. L., and N. H. Hornberger, eds. 1996. *Sociolinguistics and language teaching*. New York: Cambridge University Press.

Ogawa, N., and J. Shabamoto Smith. 1997. The gendering of the gay male sex class: A preliminary case study based on Rasen no Sobyō. In A. Livia and K. Hall, eds., *Queerly phrased: Language, gender, and sexuality*, 402–15. New York: Oxford University Press.

Okamoto, S., and J. Shibamoto Smith. 2004. *Japanese language, gender, and ideology*. Oxford: Oxford University Press.

Tannen, D. 1990. *You just don't understand: Women and men in conversation*. New York: Ballantine.

————, ed. 1993. *Gender and conversational interaction*. New York: Oxford University Press.

Thorne, B., C. Kramarae, and N. Henley, eds. 1992. *Language, gender, and society*. Rowley, Mass.: Newbury House.

Keywords

gender dialects
language and gender

11

English spelling is hard, and it makes learning to read hard. Should we do anything about it?

Many children in the United States try for years to learn to read, and some never succeed. Educators talk about a fourth-grade reading level as a milestone in the process of achieving literacy. The accepted wisdom is that once students reach this level, they cross over from learning to read to reading to learn. So, on average, it seems to take four years of schooling (not including kindergarten or pre-K education) to gain such proficiency. Gaining analogous levels of proficiency in writing skills takes even longer.

The stumbling blocks in achieving literacy in English are numerous, and many people have called for spelling reform. Instances of rebellion against traditional spelling are often used in advertising, like *lite* for *light*. Chat rooms on the Internet have something we can already call a tradition of simplified spellings. Indeed, they make use of acronyms that (for most of us) exist only as spellings, such as *brb* for *be right back*. Simplified spelling is also used in text messaging on cell phones. We can expect more as technology advances, and we can expect these simplified spellings to creep into other contexts. So here I want to ask whether spelling reform would be beneficial in all contexts, not just in these special ones in which the length of the message (as in the case of a cell phone) is an issue.

Let's look at some problems in the present spelling system. English is riddled with contrasts, such as these:

bait, wait (*not* *bate, *wate)
late, date (*not* *lait, *dait)

Here a given sound is spelled in two ways. (This particular sound is a diphthong, or what many grammar school teachers would call a long vowel.) A given sound is often spelled in multiple ways. For vowel sounds, simply identify rhyming words whose spelling differs on the rhymed portions of the words, as in the preceding examples. English has many such words, some of which are homonyms (words with identical sounds but different meanings) that are spelled differently:

beech, beach
bare, bear
sight, cite, site

There are just as many multiple spellings for consonant sounds. The initial sound in each of the following paired words is identical, but the initial letter of the words in the pairs differs:

celery, salt
flame, phlegm
judge, gesture

To complicate matters further, a given letter or series of letters can represent multiple sounds. Thus, the initial letters in each of the following paired words is identical, but the words start with different sounds:

Consonants:
celery, cool
sugar, salt
go, ginger
Vowels:
oh, on

am, all
eat, ever

In addition, a given letter or series of letters can represent no sound at all:

*k*nee
wa*l*k
veg*e*table
clim*b*
requir*e* (*contrast to* choir)

As if homonyms weren't confusing enough, English also has homographs (words with identical spelling but different meanings), which sound different:

read (as in "Let's read"), read (as in "I've read it")
lead (as in "Lead me"), lead (as in "Lead pipes break")

Examples like these enormously complicate the task of achieving literacy. It's no wonder American children (as well as children and adults anywhere who are learning to read English) take years to acquire adequate skills in reading and even more years to produce reasonably accurate spelling.

Italian children have an easier task because the correspondence between the way one pronounces a word in standard Italian and the way one spells that word is much closer to a one-to-one relationship than it is in English. The concept of a spelling bee in Italy would be ridiculous. (Nonetheless, the matter is complicated if the person who is learning to read does not have the standard pronunciation. I return to this point later.)

Our spelling system may well be a culprit in illiteracy, which is a persistent and growing problem in the United States. Although it is difficult to measure illiteracy accurately, given that there's a continuum of skills to evaluate, a 1992 National Adult Literacy Survey funded by the National Center for Education Statistics of the federal government and conducted by the Educational Testing Service (of Princeton, N.J.) found that 21–23 percent of our overall population has only the lowest level of literacy (level 1). That level 1 percentage is higher in the elderly (44–53 percent of adults sixty-five and over), a fact that might suggest that our younger population is doing better. However, the rate at level 1 is also higher in people with at most eight years of education (79 percent) and higher in people from certain ethnic groups (38–43 percent of African Americans, roughly 50 percent of the various Latino groups, and 30–36 percent of Asians). Moreover, people who scored in level 1 tended to be poor (44 percent were below the poverty line). Since the percentages of both minorities and poor people are rising, it's no surprise that illiteracy rates are also rising.

Given the problems with English spelling and the fact that illiteracy has serious societal repercussions, one might propose a spelling reform along the following lines. Adopt a writing system (such as the Roman alphabet, the system English presently uses) in which each letter represents precisely one sound, make sure that the system has a unique symbol for every sound that occurs in the language, and revise the spelling of all words accordingly. With these changes, a new reader has to learn only the association between each symbol in the writing system and each sound in the language. Once that is learned, reading is easy.

Although this sounds like a good plan with many obvious advantages, it has serious problems. Let's say we're going to adopt this system, and, for the sake of expediency and effectiveness of presentation, I'm going to suppose that you have given my husband the privilege of deciding which writing system we will adopt. I know this is arbitrary, but as a linguist I would have chosen the International Phonetic Alphabet—the system that linguists worldwide use when transcribing human languages. If I did that, however, you would have a lot of difficulty in following the examples I give. Instead, I can make the same points by using my husband's choice (most likely the same choice most readers would have made)—the Roman alphabet.

To start our discussion, I'll choose as an example a word that you might never have worried about spelling correctly because it seems so simple. However, the spelling reform we are considering here would affect every single word, no matter how simple it might seem. I'll spell a short word—one that begins with a single consonant sound, has a single vowel sound, and ends in a single consonant sound: *car*. Because we must assign a unique sound to each letter of the alphabet and a unique letter of the alphabet to each sound, it really doesn't matter at the outset what any of these assignments are. For the sake of familiarity with the old spelling system, I decide that the new spelling of *car* is "c-a-r" (that is, identical to the old spelling).

Now, however, things get tricky. I have a friend who says the word differently from me. In her speech the word "car," spoken in isolation (i.e., spoken as just a single word utterance) does not end in a consonant but a vowel. So if she were deciding the new spelling for that pronunciation, she would choose "c-a."

Another friend pronounces this word in yet a third way. She not only has no final consonant but also has a vowel distinct from mine. She has the same vowel sound in *car* that she has in *cat*. Let me arbitrarily decide to use the letter "e" for the vowel sound in *cat*. So if this friend of mine were deciding the new spelling, she would choose "c-e."

I'm very sorry to report to you that I have another friend who pronounces the word in a fourth way. Whereas I say *car* with a puff of air immediately after the first consonant, he does not. We have different pronunciations. If our spelling system is supposed to give enough information so that readers can pronounce every word in a unique way once they understand the correspondence between letters and sounds, my friend would have chosen a different spelling for *car*—one I won't even try to guess.

I won't try guessing because there is no letter of the Roman alphabet that English now uses (in the present spelling system) for the sound represented by the letter "c" of *car* that is not also used for my third friend's "c" sound. So the best bet here is to use some new letter. In fact, there are many more sounds in English than there are letters in the Roman alphabet. Consider the words *thigh* and *thy*. The sequence of letters "th" is used for two different sounds in these words, and there is no single letter in the Roman alphabet that we use for either of these sounds. Such facts mean that we will have to augment the letters of the Roman alphabet with additional symbols in our new spelling if we are to maintain the goal of having a one-to-one correspondence between sounds and letters. Since I don't want to go into the question of what new symbols we might add, I will simply leave you with the recognition of that need.

Returning to our discussion of the varying pronunciations, we face a thorny question: Whose speech should I use to determine the new spelling of the word *car*? Although I've given only four pronunciations, there are many other possibilities even for very simple words like *car*. You make use of that fact whenever you mimic an accent. If you are convinced that your own speech is standard, compare your own pronunciation of several words to those listed as preferred in a dictionary. Look up, for example, the following words:

affluent caught dog garage pen police

Language variation, especially when viewed in the context of spelling reform, brings us face to face with issues of standardization. If you accept my pronunciation of the word *car* as standard, my friends have what you might consider nonstandard pronunciations. The third friend's pronunciation may even seem un-American despite the fact that he was born and reared in the United States and has been speaking English all his life. However, in the parts of the country that my friends come from (I have lived in Boston, and I grew up in Miami) and in their social class, their speech is standard. Moreover, although my third friend's pronunciation is undoubtedly the influence of being reared by Cuban parents in a Cuban American community, many of his friends have similar pronunciations whether or not they happen to speak Spanish, which means his speech is quite standard for some of the circles he travels in.

There's no way around it: These four variations on the pronunciations of this one simple word are produced by native speakers of English. Consequently, there is no linguistic yardstick for spelling reform that would allow us to choose among them. (To understand that last claim, see chapter 8.)

In matters of choosing a standard, then, nonlinguistic factors will have to prevail. But the question is, what do we use? Geographic information probably comes to mind first, especially after the preceding examples, since most of us can easily recognize speech patterns from other areas.

We can begin by focusing on an area of high-density population as our geographic standard. There are many to choose from, but I'll choose Brooklyn because people often talk about a Brooklyn accent. How will the aspiring readers from Atlanta, with their southern accent, be aided in their quest for literacy if the words they read are spelled in a way consistent with the pronunciation of people from Brooklyn?

Even if proponents of spelling reform are not discouraged by that question, there are still other questions ahead. For one, which pronunciation of Brooklyn will we choose? Not every native speaker brought up in Brooklyn speaks the same variety of English. We could again choose on the basis of population density and ask which socioeconomic class is most prevalent: upper class, middle class, lower class, or one of the hybrids. No matter which class we choose, however, aspiring readers from the other classes will be at a disadvantage vis-à-vis spelling reform.

The matter of whose speech we select as standard (to use as the basis for spelling reform) is important because the final determination of a standard will have undeniable effects on the degree to which the spelling reform aids literacy, and it may have effects as well on the self-esteem of aspiring readers whose speech varies significantly from the chosen standard.

Nevertheless, let's assume that we somehow manage to overcome the difficulties presented by both geographic and socioeconomic variation. Now another huge problem comes up when we consider all speakers of English, not just American ones. How will children in some Welsh village fare if they try to read an American newspaper that uses this spelling reform? What about a child from Perth, Australia; Churchill, Canada; Calcutta, India; or Johannesburg, South Africa? Children in all of these places speak English, but they all have different pronunciations. Today, although there are British editions of some American works and vice versa, generally the spelling differences between the two editions are minor. People anywhere who speak English and are literate can read materials written in English, no matter who wrote them. If the United States instituted a spelling reform of the type we've been discussing, this would change. In addition, if the other English-speaking countries instituted their own spelling reforms, they would surely not choose the same pronunciation that Americans would. Thus, literature written in English in a spelling-reform world would be of varying accessibility to speakers of English, based on the particular variety of English they speak.

Let's pursue this issue of accessibility. Can you read Shakespeare? Can you read a first folio of *Romeo and Juliet*, for example, and understand it? Even if you've never tried to do this before, I expect that you can. There are different dates for this play (1591 and 1596–1597), but it is clear that it is more than four hundred years old. Assuming that the people who determined standard spelling when printing first became widespread were not trying to confound us all (a normal assumption), we can conclude that English spelling in the late 1500s had a better correspondence to pronunciation than it does today. This means that if we were to hear the words as people in Shakespeare's time actually said them, we would have considerably more difficulty in understanding the play. Still, even though the pronunciation of English has changed drastically since that time, the spelling in Shakespeare's originals is close enough to today's spelling that, with some work and strong motivation, not only scholars but also ordinary literate people have access to the folio editions of the plays.

Consider these famous lines from the second act:

O Romeo, Romeo, wherefore art thou Romeo?
828: Denie thy Father and refuse thy name:
829: Or if thou wilt not, be but sworne to my Loue,
830: And Ile no longer be a Capulet.

A literate person in the new spelling-reform age—whom I will call a new reader—not knowing how to read the old spelling system, would pronounce the words in a way that is consistent with the new spelling. Let's look at line 828 (the line in which the spelling is closest to today's). The new reader wouldn't be reading the line in the way you read it right now, with your pronunciation, but would see each letter as a symbol that has a unique sound because that's the way our new spelling-reform system is set up. The first word, *denie*, would probably have three syllables because there are three vowel letters: "e," "i," and "e," and the first and last syllables would rhyme because they'd have the same vowel sound. This pronunciation is far from how one says the word today. The second word would start with two consonant sounds because "t" and "h" would each correspond to a single consonant sound. In addition, if in our new spelling system the "t" symbol corresponded to the initial sound in *to* and the "h" corresponded to the initial sound in *hat*, the word *thy* would start with the consonant "t" followed by "h," a sequence of sounds that is not found at the start of syllables in English today. The sounds the new reader would glean from the old spelling would cause serious difficulties in recognizing the words and seriously compromise the person's appreciation of the play, to say the least.

One way to make Shakespeare accessible to the new reader, of course, is to teach that person both the new and the old spelling, but then what has spelling reform accomplished? The whole point was to make it easier to develop literacy skills. If everyone has to learn two spelling systems, literacy becomes harder to achieve. Nevertheless, let's assume we can deal with English literary tradition, and let's also say that we have wonderful new writers in this age of spelling reform.

Now jump ahead four centuries (i.e., as far forward in time as Shakespeare is behind us). Because language changes, people will undoubtedly be speaking English differently four hundred years from now. Although some language communities are more innovative in certain areas of grammar than others, language changes over time in every community. Perhaps speakers four centuries into the future will have adopted spelling reform again. These readers of the second spelling reform, whom I'll call the newest readers of the newest spelling, will have the same trouble reading our texts today in the new spelling as the new reader had reading Shakespeare in the old spelling. That is, the newest readers, if they want to read literature written in the new spelling, will have to learn new spelling, as well as the newest spelling. Furthermore, if they want to read Shakespeare, they'll have to learn the old spelling, too. Literary traditions—as we look both ahead and behind—would be seriously threatened by spelling reform.

In sum, spelling reform would probably not enhance the literacy of most aspiring readers of English (especially if we think in worldwide terms), and it would cut today's speakers off from their literary traditions.

These problems are practical in nature, and in some ways they are more sociological problems than language problems per se. Nonetheless, some strictly language problems would arise from spelling reform as well. For example, consider sets of words like the following:

electric electricity electrician

The second instance of the letter "c" in the first word corresponds to the initial sound in *car*; in the second word, to the initial sound in *salt*; and in the third word, to the initial sound in *sugar*. In the new spelling, these three separate consonant sounds would have to be spelled with three separate letters, thus obfuscating the fact that this particular consonant (no matter how it sounds in each of the three words) is part of the same word unit in all three examples. With our present spelling, however, that fact is obvious. In general, our present spelling tends to make many such connections apparent, and they would be lost with spelling reform. Moreover, literacy might actually be impeded because recognizing connections between words helps us not only to guess at the meanings of unfamiliar words but also to appreciate the interrelatedness of our vocabulary.

A staunch proponent of spelling reform might question whether the theoretical problems I've raised actually cause problems. Languages that have a written form, unless it was adopted in very recent times, have experienced writing changes. So what's wrong with spelling reform in actual practice?

Typically, writing changes have come about gradually. Some of the oldest writing systems were ideographs—essentially pictures that stood for whole words. Chinese characters originated in this way, although through stylization over the centuries they are far from iconic today:

月   moon
木   tree
新   new

Character systems often change into another type of system, one that is based on the sounds in the word. One kind is called a syllabary, in which each symbol represents a syllable of sound rather than a whole word. So a word that consists of one syllable is written with a single symbol, a word that consists of two syllables is written with two symbols, a word that consists of three syllables is written with three symbols, and so on. Cuneiform, the writing system of the ancient Sumerians, was a syllabary that developed from a character system. Neo-Assyrian was a later stage in the evolution of this writing system.

		Archaic Uruk ca. 3000	Presargonic Lagash, ca. 2400	Neo-Assyrian ca. 700
DU	'to go'			
UD₅	'goat'			
GUD	'bull'			

Modern Japanese has a mixed system. It has both characters and two different writing systems that are similar to syllabaries but differ in that light syllables are represented by a single symbol (as in ordinary syllabaries) and heavy syllables are represented by two symbols. A light syllable ends in a single short vowel (which is the most common type of syllable in Japanese). All other syllables are heavy; that is, they contain a long vowel or a diphthong and/ or end in one or more consonants. This type of writing system— based on syllable weight—is much more frequently found than are syllabaries.

| **わたし** | I | (pronounced *watashi*, written here in the Japanese system called hiragana) |
| **フランス** | France | (pronounced *Furansu*, written here in the Japanese system called katakana) |

The third major type of writing system is very familiar to you— alphabets. For several examples of different types of writing systems, visit the website http://www.omniglot.dabsol.co.uk/language/.

Over time, alphabets have prevailed for very good reasons. With a character system, every word is represented by a different symbol. In fact, some say you need to know around four thousand

Chinese characters in order to read a newspaper with adequate understanding. Think how much schooling it takes to learn four thousand characters. With a syllabary system, every distinct syllable requires a symbol. With three letters of the Roman alphabet— "a," "s," and "p"—I can spell fifteen words of English, all of which consist of only a single syllable:

a, as, ass, asp, asps
sap, saps, spa, spas, sass
pa, pas, pap, paps, pass

However, we would need fifteen different symbols to render these fifteen different syllables in a syllabary system.

Alphabets, then, are the most efficient writing systems in that the fewest number of symbols is needed to render all of the words of a language. Consequently, when a language community with some other writing system comes into contact with a language community that uses an alphabet, often the alphabet is adopted, typically with some changes to deal with differences between the sound systems of the two languages. And with the spread of alphabetic writing systems comes literacy for the common people since they can become literate with many fewer years of schooling.

Sometimes countries have resisted such changes, however, for reasons that are nonlinguistic. In 1446, for example, a Korean committee appointed by the king introduced an alphabet called the *hangul*. The king's goal was to encourage literacy among the common people. After his death, the medieval mandarins of Korea banned this alphabet precisely because they wanted to keep literacy from the common people. It wasn't until four centuries later that economic, political, and religious considerations revived *hangul*.

Indeed, religious considerations are often relevant to the ease with which linguistic communities accept writing system changes or the strength with which they resist them. Some scripts are associated with religious or cultural traditions and as such are preserved. Arabic script is associated with Islam; Hebrew script with Judaism; the Roman alphabet with Catholicism and Protestantism; the Cyrillic alphabet with the Orthodox Church; and so on. When attempts are made to revise scripts with associations of such great importance, the ensuing controversies can be heated.

In 1991 the government of Azerbaijan, recently independent from the Soviet Union, decided to change the officially recognized script from Cyrillic to Roman (adding to our twenty-six-letter alphabet to reach thirty-two letters). Since Russian is written in Cyrillic, this change was like a banner of independence and opened up an orthographic can of worms. Azerbaijan is a country with ties to Russia, Iran (which uses the Arabic alphabet with certain modifications), and Turkey (which uses the Roman alphabet). Two decades later these three alphabets exist side by side, with the Azerbaijani language written in all three. The choice of which alphabet an individual uses has less (or maybe nothing) to do with the languages of Russian, Farsi, and Turkish and more to do with cultural and political ideology. That is, which country you orient yourself toward personally is relevant and more influential than linguistic considerations alone. Scholars argue over which is best. Many want Arabic to prevail because much of Azerbaijan's traditional literature is in Arabic and because many of its people are Muslim. Others see the Roman alphabet as an important economic and political tie to the West. Still others see maintaining Cyrillic as a way to ease the transition from their Soviet past. The debate continues, and in the meantime both new and old readers—to say nothing of tourists—flounder.

In 1998 Germany adopted a spelling reform that in a few short years led to such acrimony that some states within Germany rejected it and the country was in a state of orthographic civil disorder for a while. A number of difficult questions arose: What should publishers do? What should teachers do? What impact does this have on the child who is trying to learn to read?

Sudden writing changes by decree (as in Azerbaijan and Germany), rather than gradual writing changes by differences in needs and habits, are generally painful and rarely totally success-ful (in Germany, things seem to have settled now, but it wasn't an easy process). A spelling reform of English has little chance of faring better. Certainly, the attempts of the American Philological Association, the British Spelling Reform Association, the (Ameri-can) National Education Association, and the Simplified Spelling Board from the latter half of the 1800s through the first half of the 1900s met insuperable resistance.

Although I conclude that spelling reform is not a good idea, literacy rates in the United States are deplorable. We must do something about it—for without an education, the future of any individual is unpromising. Unfortunately, there is no quick fix. The whole idea of spelling reform is at first attractive, I believe, because it would be so convenient to have a quick remedy. Who doesn't feel sympathy for the new reader who is facing the regretta-ble spelling of words like *neighbor* and *phlegm*? Nonetheless, spell-ing reform will not help literacy in the long run.

The answers to our literacy problems will take work, but I, like many other educators, have one answer to offer: Read to chil-dren. Go into schools and volunteer your time. Show children that there is a reason to go through all the work of learning to read. Offer them the joy of good books. Start with the very young, but don't ignore teens or, for that matter, adults who are struggling with literacy. In my experience, it works.

Further Reading

Daniels, P., and W. Bright, eds. 1996. *The world's writing systems*. New York: Oxford University Press.

Diringer, D. 1948. *The alphabet: A key to the history of mankind*. New York: Philosophical Library.

Eszett, D. German spelling reform and double-s words. http://german.about.com/homework/german/library/weekly/aa092898.htm (accessed May 3, 2009).

Gaur, A. 1984. *A history of writing*. London: British Library.

Keywords

English spelling
spelling reform
writing systems

12

Should the United States adopt English as the official language and overhaul the educational system accordingly?

The English Only Movement (EOM) has among its goals an adoption of English as the official language of the United States. Because the EOM is a strong and vocal movement in many states, it is important to face this proposal, but to do so, we have to understand exactly what it means for a language to be "official." Then we can consider its effects on schools. While the following discussion concerns the situation in the United States, many countries today have linguistically pluralistic societies, so analogous issues arise elsewhere.

The two largest groups that support the EOM are the U.S. English Foundation and English First. The former, with a membership of more than one million, wants (among other things) improved education in English for immigrants in order to enhance their economic opportunities. English First, with only around 150,000 members, wants (among other things) to have English declared the one and only official language of the United States.

The goal of the U.S. English Foundation—that of enhancing economic opportunities for immigrants—when used as motivation for the EOM reveals the assumption that there is a cause-and-effect relationship between what language a person is educated in and the extent to which that person is economically stigmatized. Immigrants typically move into poor neighborhoods, and their children often attend underfunded schools. Underfunded schools, regardless of whether or not they teach only in English, tend to produce students who are less prepared for the job market. Without a way to pry apart the effects of underfunding from those of the language(s) of instruction, the cause-and-effect relationship that the EOM assumes cannot be maintained.

If the EOM were successful and English became the only official language of the United States, all federal activities would take place exclusively in English. This would include anything pertaining to national elections, such as information on candidates and voting procedures, and all evidentiary and informational matter in a federal legal proceeding. Under our present laws, citizenship via naturalization does not require English literacy for people who have lived in the United States for twenty years or more or for people over the age of fifty. The impact on the federal legal rights of these naturalized citizens is obvious. Moreover, in the 1984 presidential election, 77 percent of the Spanish-speaking voters that needed bilingual ballots were born in the United States. The adoption of English as the official language, then, would affect the voting rights of many citizens. A change in voter turnout could also have drastic effects on the political climate of the country, thus touching the lives of all of its citizens.

If states were to follow suit and adopt English as their official language, all state activities would take place exclusively in English, including all matters pertaining to departments of motor vehicles. Thus, we should review the stated goals of the EOM and ask ourselves how the inability to get a driver's license will enhance the economic opportunities of non-English speakers. I'm hoping to impress on you the discrepancy between the stated goals of the EOM and their probable outcomes, at least in the short term. You can go one by one through other privileges on the federal, state, and local levels to realize the impact of such a change both on individuals and on society as a whole.

Through the Voting Rights Act of 1965, the federal government took action to protect civil rights regardless of one's language. On August 11, 2000, President Clinton strengthened these efforts by signing an executive order directing federal agencies to "improve the language-accessibility of their programs" by December 11, 2000. The EOM works indirectly against the act of 1965 and directly against the act of 2000.

Does the EOM aim to rob some citizens of their civil rights, as well as other benefits? If we can judge from the publications and activities of the movement, the answer is no. (See www.usenglish. org/inc/official/about/why.asp). Instead, this unfortunate result is incidental to its main goals.

Rather, the EOM's primary target for reform is the educational system. So let's consider a crucial aspect of education: funding. It is possible that if English became the official language of the United States, only those schools that adopted English as their only language of instruction and business (excluding instruction in foreign language) would receive federal tax dollars, and in states that adopted English as the official language, it is possible that only those same schools would receive state tax dollars, and on it goes—down to the local tax level. Schools with a significant number of students who speak a language other than English and decide to allow (or even encourage) bilingual education might be severely underfunded.

Because education is the target of the EOM and because the use of language in education is something linguistics can help us understand, I want to address at length the question of whether instruction solely in English, in all classes other than foreign language classes, would improve conditions in the United States. First, however, I briefly examine what could be some unstated motivations of the EOM.

One might be patriotism, which could be expected to figure prominently, particularly since the acts of terrorism of September 11, 2001. Aside from language, several different ways in which culture related to family origins can be expressed include food (probably foremost) and then (in no particular order) religion, music, child-rearing habits, dancing, appreciation of certain types of art, decoration of home and self, and superstitions. Is there any necessary relationship between these things and a person's patriotism? Surely Americans must answer no. Americans value a multicultural society, which America has been since its inception. It is significant that there isn't any movement to reduce the types of food enjoyed in the United States, the different religions practiced, the styles and traditions of music produced and listened to, and so on. Why should language be singled out from other cultural habits?

This brings us to what could be a second unstated motivation of the EOM: a country in which everyone understands each other perfectly. At first glance it seems patently obvious that if everyone speaks a single language, miscommunications won't occur. A second glance reveals the error in this. Most divorces are not between people of different native languages, yet miscommunication is a commonly cited grievance between parting spouses. Also consider ordinary, daily situations—not ones like lovers' spats, which are highly charged emotionally and thus might be more susceptible to miscommunication. For example, I was peppering a sauce, and my daughter Eva said to me, "You can't add too much pepper." Now what did she mean? Was she warning me not to add any more pepper? Or was she encouraging me to make it spicy? The two readings of this sentence are contradictory. My daughter didn't intend to confound me, but she did.

Miscommunication is common even among speakers who share a native language, and some would question whether perfect understanding is possible among humans. If two people do not have a rudimentary knowledge of a lingua franca, they will be hampered in communication, but a rudimentary knowledge is a far cry from a command of the language that enables a person to use it for all civil rights and educational matters.

Therefore, if either patriotism or the desire for a country in which everyone understands everyone else perfectly is a motive behind the EOM, it is misguided. Worse yet, the EOM might reinforce and exaggerate the very inequities it aims to correct.

Now it's time to face the major target of the EOM: language in education. Let's begin with a historical perspective. In colonial America, settlers came from England, of course, but many also came from other European countries, and some came from African countries. In addition, the indigenous people remained to varying degrees. Thus, America has been a multilingual nation since its inception.

Bilingualism and trilingualism (and more) were common practices in the colonial classroom. By the end of the 1600s, bilingual English-German classrooms were found throughout the colonies, and instruction in both languages persisted through the mid-1800s.

Controversy over which languages should be used for instruction started at least as early as the American Revolution, when Benjamin Franklin, among others, worried that the use of German might weaken national unity and hinder government proceedings. Nevertheless, bilingual instruction continued in an atmosphere of general political detachment and tolerance.

Increased immigration of Germans in the mid- to late 1800s led to a newly energized debate over bilingual education. Again the debate centered mostly around whether people who spoke a language other than English could be good citizens, not whether instruction in a language other than English could be effective educational policy. With World War I, anti-German sentiments nearly kept German from being a possible language of instruction in the United States.

Just as English-German bilingualism was commonplace in the colonial classrooms, so was English-Spanish bilingualism in California classrooms in the 1800s. However, the mass immigration of Mexicans, because of the gold rush, quickly led to anti-Mexican sentiments, and in 1855 California banned Spanish as a language of instruction. Later, changes in the laws allowed bilingual education to become more common again in the second half of the 1900s.

Now the EOM threatens to end such instruction and has already started its campaign in California. The passage in 1998 of Proposition 227 mandates changes in the educational system, one of which is that students with limited English proficiency (LEP) be segregated from native English speakers and taught almost exclusively in English before being moved into regular classes. The term for this practice is "sheltered English immersion." The proponents of P227 claimed that this kind of immersion is more effective in teaching English language skills than simply placing LEP students in curricula designed for native English speakers— what can be called submersion—and more effective than bilingual classrooms.

The EOM is right that submersion doesn't work well. In the early 1900s, immigrants who were thrown into classrooms with native English speakers and were not given any special linguistic aids did not do well academically. A 1911 study by the U.S. Immigration Service reported that 77 percent of Italian, 60 percent of Russian, and 51 percent of German immigrant children lagged a grade or more behind in school as compared to 28 percent of native-born white children (www.aclu.org/library/pbp6. html). Native-born African American children were not included in the study.

On the other hand, it is difficult to determine whether bilingual education in the United States has fared any better. Studies of the progress of LEP students mix data on children in English as a Second Language (ESL) programs with those on children in true bilingual programs. The ESL programs offer special instruction in English language skills but often place the children in regular classrooms for the rest of their studies. These are, then, submersion programs with English language instruction on the side. True bilingual programs offer instruction in both languages in alternating patterns.

Therefore, the real question is whether the immersion or the bilingual classroom is a more effective approach to the education of children whose native language is not English.

As of this writing, it appears that P227 has not achieved its stated goal. The National Literacy Panel on Language-minority Children and Youth Report 2006 states that children in both elementary and secondary schools instructed in both Spanish and English (where Spanish is their first language) score better on reading tests than children instructed only in English. Their conclusion is that literacy in a first language (here Spanish) enhances literacy in a second (here English). This finding is in accord with what linguists and educators have been saying for years: Children most easily learn to read and write in a language they know well. Furthermore, they master content material (science, math, history, etc.) better if the material is presented in a language they know well. Finally, good literacy skills in a first language are the best predictors of good literacy skills in a second. So children who begin their education in their native language are primed to learn well in a second language later on.

These claims predicted that bilingual education would be more successful than immersion—and the 2006 study suggests they were right.

That's just one study, though. We might want to wait for the results of additional ones before we make our own judgment here, but we cannot afford to wait. There is a lot of personal wealth behind the EOM, and it is funding drives for propositions similar to California's P227 in other states and nationally. (The most recent, as of this writing, was in Nashville, Tennessee, in January 2009, which was voted down.) So, based on our own experience, let's try to answer the question of whether an immersion or a bilingual classroom is preferable.

Pretend you are a small child who is entering school. You are handed a beautiful book. You open it up and see:

ἀγαθὸς ὁ ἄνθρωπος

You might exclaim, "This is Greek to me! It's not even the Roman alphabet." Well, you're right. This is ancient Greek, and your reaction helps me to make an important point. If I gave you a passage written in the Roman alphabet, even if you didn't know the language, you'd know how to at least begin to pronounce the passage simply because you read English. Read this aloud:

Vi er her kun tre dage.

You are probably not pronouncing it exactly as a native speaker of that language (Danish) pronounces it, but you're probably not wildly off either. (This sentence means 'We're here for only three days.')

It's hard for us to simulate the experience of a child who is entering school because you already know what reading is. You know that the letters on the page correspond to sounds and that the sounds go together to form words. A child who is learning to read has to first learn that correspondence. It's important, then, to strip away whatever advantages you have over immigrant children to really understand the task in front of them.

Here's our situation: We are American children whose native language is English. We have moved to some mythical land where people speak ancient Greek. We are now in school and enrolled in an immersion program. We have to master the writing system, and at the same time we have to master the new language. (Let's be grateful that we already know what reading entails.)

So with all that in mind, the line in front of us is, once more:

ἀγαθὸς ὁ ἄνθρωπος

What does it mean? How can we figure it out? The teacher points to the printed page and says something. Maybe it sounds something like this to our ears:

ahgatoshoantropos

Lots of things are odd about these sounds. First, there's a pitch change on the boldfaced sounds (the first "o" and the third "a"), but that changing pitch is not accompanied by extra loudness or length, unlike stress in English. Second, the "r" sound is trilled, unlike in English. Third, the vowels aren't exactly the same as English vowels.

We see the letters and hear the sentence, but we don't know which sounds correspond to which letters on the page. (If we didn't know what reading was, we wouldn't even know that we're supposed to discern such a correspondence.) We don't know from the sounds where the word breaks are because the speech stream of an utterance simply doesn't give that information.

Realizing that we are lost, the teacher may pronounce the words again—slowly. What would you do if you were the teacher? Say the following English sentence in a casual way:

This is going to be interesting.

Now pretend you are a teacher who is trying to help a child learn to read. Say the sentence again, this time taking care to pronounce each written syllable in a way that is close to the spelling. Unless you are highly unusual, you pronounced *interesting* differently the second time, and probably your pronunciation of *going to be* was different as well.

Most likely our teacher of ancient Greek did the same—the first pronunciation would have been different from the second. Although trying to help, the teacher is giving the child two different pronunciations of the same letters on the page. These good intentions aren't making the child's job any easier. All the child can do is mimic like a trained parrot.

The teacher moves on to the next sentence:

τὰ τοῦ ἀνθρωπου παιδιὰ καλα

And on to the next, which I won't even write because by this point we, the immigrant children, are desperately seeking any source of help. Perhaps our teacher looks at us with annoyance, interpreting our wandering eyes as evidence that we aren't paying attention. We're starting out on the wrong foot. A teacher's early impression is not easily overcome. Plus, like other children, we are aware of how teachers view us. We wonder whether school is a nice place or not.

The reading lesson finally ends, and, being immigrants, we are sent to a special support class (as in the P227 model). Our special language teacher knows some English, although she doesn't sound much like we do. She looks at our reading book and says over and over again that the first sentence means "The man is good." When we look at her with blank faces, she realizes that we don't know what reading entails or even what the linguistic unit of a word is, so she explains.

Now we are more confused than ever. The English translation has four words, but the Greek has only three. Our special language teacher tells us that the Greek word for 'is' doesn't have to be written and that this is just a difference between Greek and English.

We point to the first word and say, "the"; to the second, and say, "man"; to the third—but before we can speak, the special language teacher stops us. It seems that the first word means 'good'; the second word means 'the'; and the third means 'man.' She tells us that words can come in many orders in ancient Greek, so we try the following order:

ὁ ἄνθρωπος ἀγαθός

The teacher smiles in approval. Now we try this order:

ἄνθρωπος ὁ ἀγαθός

The teacher stops smiling. This order is no good because the word for 'the' must come before the word for 'man'—because, she tells us, that's just how it is. I could go on, but you're probably already sick of this example, and the child you were pretending to be is probably sick of it, too.

The list of the things that child has to learn includes (1) the letters, (2) the correspondence between letters and sounds, (3) the linguistic notion of words, and (4) the Greek language—with its different sounds and different syntax. It's a daunting list.

Now face one more fact: The little immigrant children, the children we were pretending to be, are marched back to the regular classroom. They now face science, history, geography, and math—all taught in Greek.

Certainly learning Greek is not confined to the classroom. The child picks up words on the playground and in the lunch-room, although many words that come up in the subjects stud-ied in school are not used in these other places. Certain words are restricted to academic settings—like *photosynthesis*—so all of the children in the classroom are learning these words for the first time. The immigrant child is simply learning them in Greek rather than in English. However, other classroom words are part of our ordinary vocabulary, like *country* (in a geography lesson), *liver* (in a science lesson), and so on. Here the immigrant child has to do more work than the other children because the others already know the Greek word. That is, immigrant children struggle with language acquisition on top of subject material for a long, long time—for years, in fact, because the task is huge.

Let's now pretend to be children in a bilingual English-Greek program, which is organized in the following way. Each bilingual classroom has two teachers. Both are bilingual, but one is English dominant (English is her native language), and one is Greek domi-nant. The teachers teach in their dominant language (one teaches in English; the other in Greek), although they listen and respond to questions in either language. They take turns teaching the subjects: If one teaches math one day, the other will teach math the next. We, the children, hear, discuss, and read and write about all of the subjects in both languages. When the teacher teaches in our native language, we have just as much chance of learning as we would in a school in our native country, and we are still exposed to all of the material in the other language that the child in the immersion program is exposed to.

Now let's pretend we are children who enter a differently organized bilingual English-Greek program. In this school, children are taught all of the subjects in their native language through the fourth grade, with the addition of intensive language courses in the other language. Then, in the fifth grade, they are put into classrooms that use the model described in the preceding paragraph. This particular school then moves to a regular Greek program in the ninth grade. Thus, we children learn just as much as we would have learned in our native country through the fourth grade, at which point our literacy skills are well developed. Now we move into the fifth grade, and our task is simply to learn the subject matter, not to learn both a new language and a subject matter at the same time. Then in the ninth grade, we change to an all-Greek program, but our skills in our native language are so good that we can keep reading and writing in it for the rest of our lives. This model, unlike the first one, presents problems for students who are transferring into the program, problems that we would expect to be more severe the older the transfer students are. Its advantage, however, is that it exploits the fact that children gain literacy in a second language faster and more thoroughly if they are already literate in their first.

There are other models for bilingual programs, but I've given just these two because the first is one I'm familiar with (my oldest daughter attended such a school—the Oyster School in Washington, D.C.), and the second is the one I find more promising. I myself would be more likely to thrive in some variety of bilingual program than in an immersion program.

There's no doubt that bilingual education is expensive, and if the school has children from two dozen different languages, no community could afford to fully implement either model for all of them. However, many communities in the United States have a large number of speakers of a single non-English language. These are the communities that perhaps cannot afford not to implement an effective bilingual program.

At this point I want to turn us briefly to issues of language policy and Deaf people since the literacy rate for this population has been persistently low for more than a century and since the factors that have negatively impacted the literacy of Deaf people revolve around matters of bilingualism. Near the end of the nineteenth century a movement was begun to make all Deaf people use the spoken language of their country. For the United States, that meant spoken English. So let us begin with two relevant questions for the proponents of that movement: Can a Deaf person learn to speak English? Can a Deaf person learn to understand spoken English?

Many Deaf people have spent years in learning to speak English with little or no success. Some (a minority), on the other hand, have learned to speak so well that hearing strangers can often understand them. Many Deaf people have tried for years to speech-read (that is, interpret language from the movement of the lips, cheeks, jaw, etc.), with moderate or little success, although a few have had great success.

The job of a Deaf person who is learning to speak a language and speech-read is far more demanding than that of a hearing person who is learning to sign and understand sign language. Most Deaf people do not succeed—and the educational and emotional cost for those who do succeed can be very high. Since most hearing people do not sign, it is no surprise that hearing people and Deaf people generally go their separate ways when it comes to personal lives and hence have separate cultures.

That Deaf and hearing people should have separate cultures is not a problem per se. The problem is that Deaf people are precluded from the huge majority culture, and, thus, the rights of Deaf people, including their rights to education, have not been fairly protected.

Before I go into the question of language policy, however, I want to point out that Deaf people do not have to be excluded from the hearing culture. Years ago a large population of congenitally Deaf people lived on Martha's Vineyard, Massachusetts. The island responded by everyone becoming fluent in sign language.

We are now ready to discuss two important issues regarding language policy and Deaf people. One involves the right to be informed and to inform. The other involves the right to an education.

When the medical community around the world became aware of the contagious nature of AIDS, a vast public information campaign took place in many countries, but no effort was made to inform Deaf communities. As a result, AIDS spread like wildfire among Deaf communities. Who knows how long this might have gone on if it hadn't been for the activism of Harry Woosley Jr., who started the Deaf AIDS Project in 1990 (http://www.hivdent.org)? Not informing Deaf people has had catastrophic results for Deaf populations around the world.

Why did our government and our medical community ignore the rights of Deaf people? One reason is quite simple: In general Deaf people have been invisible. It is partially due to the work of linguists that they have become more visible and their rights are starting to be protected. In 1960 William Stokoe's book *Sign Language Structure* made it obvious that ASL is a natural human language. Linguists have since produced articles, books, and journals that analyze ASL and other sign languages around the world (see chapter 5).

Under the 1990 Americans with Disabilities Act, Deaf people now have the right to an interpreter in many situations, including all legal proceedings and all medical procedures, a service that is paid for by the courts and the medical profession.

The second right involves education. Before 1750, almost no deaf person in the Western world had any hope of literacy or education. However, in 1755 the Abbé de l'Epée, a cleric who was appalled by the bestial living conditions of deaf people in Paris, set up the National Institution for Deaf-Mutes. He used a combination of the signs and fingerspelling of local Deaf communities to teach them. One of the teachers at the school, the Abbé Roch-Ambroise Sicard, was particularly effective. Sicard trained his Deaf pupil Jean Massieu to be a teacher at the school, and Massieu in turn trained another Deaf pupil, Laurent Clerc, to be a teacher. In 1816 Clerc joined Thomas Gallaudet, a hearing man with a Deaf wife, and went to the United States to set up the American Asylum for the Deaf in Hartford, Connecticut. They brought with them French Sign Language (LSF), but their pupils, of course, used a variety of local sign languages and home signs (that is, signs their families had made up to communicate with them).

What's going to happen when you throw together people using mutually incomprehensible sign languages? Here we had only a couple of teachers using one sign language (LSF), and many children using different sign languages. But the two teachers had a lot of power, since they were the authorities in the classroom. The stage is set for a pidgin—a kind of slapdash contact language that will allow rudimentary communication (as discussed in chapter 9)—which is what happened at the Hartford school. But pidgins don't last. The generation of Deaf students who were exposed only to this pidgin (not to LSF or to the local sign languages) came up with a creole, what we now call ASL, which is exactly what occurs with spoken language (as discussed in chapter 9).

The success of the school in Hartford (which later changed its name to the American School for the Deaf) led Congress in 1864 to pass a law that authorized the Columbia Institution for the Deaf and Blind in Washington, D.C. This was the first institution of higher learning specifically for Deaf and blind people.

Did it make sense to put Deaf and blind people together? Are their special educational needs similar? Blind people do not form a language community, and they speak exactly like sighted people. Misconceptions about these handicaps were responsible for putting Deaf and blind people together. Nevertheless, the establishment of this institution must be applauded as a milestone. Its first principal was Edward Gallaudet, the son of Thomas, and it was later rechristened Gallaudet University. It is one of the most important educational institutions for Deaf people in the world. Many other Deaf schools were founded in multiple states.

All was going well. However, in the 1870s a debate began, for which Alexander Graham Bell was largely responsible, and resulted in a huge setback for the education of Deaf people. Bell and others argued that educating Deaf people in sign language served to isolate them from the hearing community. Therefore, Deaf people should not be allowed to sign but instead should be taught to vocalize and speech-read.

So-called oral schools then sprang up. In 1880 an international Congress of Educators of the Deaf in Milan, Italy, condemned the use of sign language in classrooms. Overnight, signing was prohibited in most classrooms in the Western world. By 1907 there were 197 schools for Deaf people in the United States, and none of them used ASL. Let's think about what it would be like to try to vocalize if you couldn't hear. Suppose that someone plugs the ears of a hearing person and then brings him to Thailand and asks him to learn to speak Thai. No aural input of Thai is available. How does he do it? If he already knows another spoken language, he has a head start, of course, because spoken languages have in common major distinctions between sounds, such as consonant sounds versus vowel sounds. He also knows that the teeth, tongue, vocal cords, lungs, oral and nasal cavities, and lips are all involved in making language sounds. But how can he learn exactly where to place his tongue in his mouth when making a sound if he cannot compare his mimicking of that sound? How can he learn exactly the right amount of tightening of his vocal cords or exactly the right amount of pressing of his lips or any number of other factors relevant to producing the quality of particular sounds without the benefit of checking his mimic against a model?

Oral schools used many methods, including rewards when the production of a word got close to the model and punishments when it didn't. Teachers put students' hands on the teachers' throats, cheeks, or lips to help them feel the external effects of what was happening inside the speech tract. The information you can gain in this way is severely limited.

What about trying to speech-read? Mouth the words *pat, bat*, and *mat* to a friend across the room. Your friend almost assuredly will not be able to distinguish among them because the differences occur inside the vocal tract at places you cannot see. With the initial sound in *pat*, the vocal cords are not vibrating rapidly, but with the initial sounds in *bat* and *mat* they are. With the initial sound in *mat*, the air flows continuously out through the nose, but with the initial sounds in *pat* and *bat* it does not. The longer the word is, the more opportunities there are for multiple readings of sounds if the only information you have comes from looking at the face of the person speaking.

In oral schools, children spent years trying to learn to vocalize and speech-read. Often they were taught very little mathematics, geography, history, or literature in an effort to teach them vocalization and speechreading instead. In other words, these schools were trying hard to essentially undo deafness rather than educate Deaf people. It's no surprise that oralism failed miserably. In the 1850s, in the heyday of Deaf education in ASL, the graduates of the Hartford asylum were as literate as the hearing population. However, by 1972, the average reading level of an eighteen-year-old Deaf high school graduate in the United States was at the fourth-grade level. A similar situation prevailed in Britain.

Today Deaf children in the United States either are enrolled in special bilingual-bicultural (ASL-English) schools for Deaf students or (in most cases) are mainstreamed into hearing schools with extra support classes and aides who interpret for them. An ideal mainstream model is far off for most school districts, though, hopefully, we are on the way to restoring to Deaf people the right to education. Still, there is a new threat to the education of Deaf people. With the growing prevalence of cochlear implants (CIs), more communities are turning back to oral programs. Recent evidence, however, suggests that children with CIs still need extra support classes, and those who are in bilingual-bicultural educational settings do better academically than those who are in strictly oral settings.

Any educational reforms—whether the EOM regarding immigrant children or the movement that Alexander Graham Bell started regarding Deaf children—affect all of us. A society in which children of any particular group receive a deficient education and possibly a negative attitude toward education risks predictable consequences. This is true whether the children have immigrant parents, are of a particular race, are Deaf, or are simply poor. Americans pride themselves on protecting one of the finest parts of their national heritage—the right to an education. Repeatedly, they have interpreted that right to mean an equal education.

Further Reading

Ambert, A. N., ed. 1988. Bilingual education and English as a second language: A research handbook, 1986–1988. New York: Garland.

August, D., and T. Shanahan, eds. 2006. *Developing literacy in second-language learners: Report of the National Literacy Panel on Language-minority Children and Youth*. Mahwah, N.J.: Erlbaum.

Baker, C., and S. P. Jones, eds. 1998. *Encyclopedia of bilingualism and bilingual education*. Philadelphia: Multilingual Matters.

Boulet, J. Jr. 2000. Clinton's tower of babble. http://www.nationalreview.com/comment/comment082300b.shtml (accessed May 3, 2009).

Cenoz, J., and F. Genesee, eds. 1998. *Beyond bilingualism: Multilingualism and multilingual education*. Philadelphia: Multilingual Matters.

Cummins, J. 1989. *Empowering minority students*. Sacramento: California Association for Bilingual Education.

Dutcher, N. 1994. *The use of first and second languages in education: A review of educational experience*. In collaboration with G. R. Tucker. Washington, D.C.: World Bank, East Asia and the Pacific Region, Country Department III.

English First. 1993. Response to questions from Senator Alan K. Simpson. U.S. Senate Committee on the Judiciary. Voting Rights Act language assistance amendments of 1992 hearing, February 26, 1992, 138–59. Washington, D.C.: U.S. Government Printing Office.

Enright, S., and M. McCloskey. 1988. *Integrating English: Developing English language and literacy in the multilingual classroom*. Reading, Mass.: Addison-Wesley.

Fisher, J. and P. Mattiacci. 2008. Civil rights in Deaf education: Working toward empowering Deaf students and their parents. In D. DeLuca, I. W. Leigh, K. A. Lindgren, and D. J. Napoli (eds.) *Access: Multiple avenues for deaf people*, 75–98. Washington, D. C.: Gallaudet University Press.

Frederickson, J., ed. 1995. *Reclaiming our voices: Bilingual education, critical pedagogy, and praxis.* Ontario: California Association for Bilingual Education.

Freeman, Y., and D. Freeman. 1992. *Whole language for second language learners.* Portsmouth, N.H.: Heinemann.

Garcia, E. 1994. *Understanding and meeting the challenge of student cultural diversity.* Boston: Houghton Mifflin.

Genesee, F. 1987. *Learning through two languages: Studies of immersion and bilingual education.* Cambridge, Mass.: Newbury House.

———, ed. 1994. *Educating second language children: The whole child, the whole curriculum, the whole community.* New York: Cambridge University Press.

HIVdent (about HIV). http://www.hivdent.org (accessed May 3, 2009).

Nussbaum, D., R. LaPorta, and J. Hinger, eds. 2002. *Cochlear implants and sign language: Putting it all together.* April 11–12, 2002, Conference Proceedings. Laurent Clerc National Deaf Education Center, Gallaudet University. http://clerccenter.gallaudet.edu/ciec/conference-proceedings.html (accessed July 25, 2008).

Oakes, J. 1985. *Keeping track: How schools structure inequality.* New Haven, Conn.: Yale University Press.

Stinson, M. 2008. Inclusion and the development of Deaf identity. In D. DeLuca, I. W. Leigh, K. A. Lindgren, and D. J. Napoli (eds.) *Access: Multiple avenues for deaf people*, 99–121. Washington, D. C.: Gallaudet University Press.

Two-way immersion. http://www.cal.org/twi/BIB.htm (accessed May 3, 2009).

Woodward, J. 1989. Some sociolinguistic aspects of French and American Sign Languages. In H. Lane and F. Grosjean (eds.) *Recent perspectives on American Sign Language*, 103–118. Mahwah, NJ: Lawrence Erlbaum Associates.

Zuckerman, M. B. 1998. The facts of life in America. *U.S. News & World Report* 1 (August 10): 68.

Keywords

bilingual education
Deaf rights

13

How does language wield power over us?
Can it overpower us?

This chapter deals with four different types of powerful or manipulative language use. I go through them one by one, in each case introducing some new terminology. The terms to look for are listed here. Since it is important for the readability of this chapter that you familiarize yourself with these terms, the definition or explanation of each one is given in boldface the first time it comes up in the discussion:

> presupposition
> entailment
> cancelability test
> conversational implicature
> frame/framing
> taboo terms

One of my favorite topics to cover in the semantics class that I teach at Swarthmore College is "presuppositions" and what happens when they are false. **A presupposition is something that speaker and listener take for granted when they produce or interpret an utterance.** The statement "He quit smoking," for example, presupposes that "he" used to smoke. You can't quit doing something that you never did. Because a presupposition has to be true if the utterance that presupposes it is true, it is called a type of **entailment. Sentence A, "He quit smoking," entails sentence**

B (its presupposition), "He used to smoke," because if A is true, B must be true as well.

To help students remember what a presupposition is, I ask them to imagine the following scenario. You are in court, being interrogated, and you are wrongly accused of beating your dog. A clever lawyer might ask you, "Have you stopped beating your dog?" If you are instructed to answer either yes or no, what would you say? If you say yes, you are asserting that you are not beating your dog now, but you are also admitting to having beaten your dog. The alternative, saying no, is even worse because now you are saying both that you are currently beating your dog and that you have beaten him in the past. So, neither yes nor no is an appropriate answer. The only way to get out of this mess is to say that you cannot answer this question because it comes with a false presupposition. You never did beat your dog, so whether you stopped cannot be an issue.

Clearly, this is a scenario in which language can overpower us. Unless the person being interrogated here knows about verbs like *quit* and *stop*, which come with a presupposition, or otherwise manages to stay calm and unintimidated enough to explain that this simply is not an appropriate question, the person is in trouble.

Similar scenarios, in which utterances come with a hidden layer of meaning, involve advertisements. Flipping through a magazine, we get bombarded with ads seemingly promising us the world. A common strategy of advertisers is to use modals (i.e., auxiliary/helping verbs) like *can* or *may*. Reading a slogan like "X can help you Y within days," where X is some product and Y is something that X is supposed to help us do, we automatically think that it actually does Y. For example, a skin care product might be marketed with the slogan "X can help your skin clear up within days." Great, you think, this is what you've been looking for. You are falling for the hidden layer of meaning, which here is the implication that product X does indeed help clear up your skin within days. Applying the so-called **cancelability diagnostic, which tests whether the meaning one would infer from an utterance is an actual, undeniable entailment or merely a conversational implicature**, we discover that product X does not promise all that much. It is perfectly fine to say the following (and I'm applying the cancelability test here):

> Product X can help clear up your skin within days, but in fact, it does not.

Although it is conversationally implicated that the product actually does help clear up your skin, that is, people read the ad and are naturally led to assume that it does, this inference the public draws can easily be canceled or denied. So, if you decide to sue the company that made the product because your skin did not improve at all, the company will probably laugh at you and say that its ad says nothing about the product actually helping. All it says is that it can help (not that it does help). On top of that, it says only that it can help, not work miracles without other measures. Moreover, "within days" doesn't even give the consumer a measurable span of time. There is no mention of a certain number of days within which the product is supposed to be effective.

Ads that say something like "If you use X, you will Y," while they do make a promise of effectiveness, employ a similar strategy because they, too, give rise to a conversational implicature, that is, they invite us to infer something that seems to hold but can easily be canceled. Let's say X is a learning aid, and Y stands for doing better in school. The slogan might read, "If you use X, your child will do better in school." If you happen to have a child that is not doing well in school and are worried that you as a parent might fail to help the child succeed, you probably read the ad and think that if you don't use X, your child won't do better in school. This is what the slogan invites us to conclude. But, again, is this implication actually entailed, or is it just conversationally implicated? Applying the cancelability test shows that, once again, the message is not as strong as it seems. It is fine to cancel the implication by saying,

> If you use X, your child will do better in school, but it is not the case that if you don't use X, your child won't do better.

There are certainly other ways that children can improve their performance in school, so parents should not feel guilty for not buying the product. Still, somehow, we do. Advertisements are devious that way.

Besides the courtroom and the world of advertising, another arena of life in which language can be unfairly manipulative is politics. Just as the question "Have you stopped beating your dog?" is impossible to answer with a simple yes or no if you have never beaten the animal, it is impossible to carry out directives like the following (I will get to examples involving political manipulation in a moment):

> Don't think of an elephant!

This is an impossible task because, in order to purposefully not think of an elephant, you, of course, have to think of an elephant. Why is that? Well, for one, **you have to interpret the words of the utterance, which include *elephant*, and in doing that you evoke a frame that includes a wide range of knowledge that comes with your understanding of what an elephant is.** So, there you are, stuck thinking about an elephant (and perhaps Africa and/or Asia and perhaps ivory poaching or animal endangerment in general and potentially many other things).

People with political agendas (of any bent) can exploit these frames to their benefit. Let's take an example that has been analyzed at great length in the literature: the term *tax relief*. Focus your attention on the word *relief* in particular. If we have relief, then we certainly have some affliction from which we are relieved, and afflictions must have people they strike: the afflicted. In addition, relief entails forces that rescue the afflicted from the affliction. This feels very much like the elements of a story in which we have a victim (the afflicted person) of a crime (the affliction) who is rescued by a hero (the source of relief). We all know crimes are bad and heroes are good, and any decent victim is grateful to a hero. So this particular frame (the tax-relief frame) sets in motion a whole scenario that we have been conditioned to respond to in certain ways.

Now, let's say you don't believe that tax cuts are beneficial, and so they cannot be a form of relief, and you are asked to defend your position. You face a difficult, if not impossible, task. So long as the term *tax relief* is used in the question, as it is here,

> Some say that more tax relief creates more jobs. You have voted against increased tax relief. Why?

the tax-relief frame will be evoked. Furthermore, even if your answer begins with an argument against the very existence of such a thing as tax relief, the very use of the words will reinforce the frame. Just as people cannot help but think of an elephant when somebody tells them not to, people cannot help but think of a crime, a victim, a hero, and so on when they hear talk about tax relief.

Moving on to another example of powerful language, **swear words like *damn* and *bastard*, so-called taboo terms,** can evoke a strong emotional reaction from people, and sometimes that reaction is not the one the speaker is seeking. Consider this example (plucked from the linguistics literature) of a school superintendent who attempted to take a stand against racism by saying in a speech,

> Niggers come in all colors. To me, a nigger is someone who doesn't respect themselves or others.

The superintendent's intentions did not include making a racial slur. Indeed, his intentions were quite the contrary—he was trying to make the point that the derogative N-word is a name that people deserve to be called if they don't show respect for themselves or others, and this holds for people of any color or race. Nonetheless, regardless of his intentions, his use of the N-word shocked people, and the community reacted with outrage, as though he had, in fact, made a racial slur.

This particular reaction—one of taking offense where none is intended—is actually fairly common, particularly when the taboo term involves race, ethnicity, a particular religion, sexual orientation, or other areas that have a history of discrimination surrounding them. Most of us know that, and we recognize that we are taking a risk if we use such terms. Some of the people who categorically refuse to use taboo terms and refuse to allow their children to use them (at least insofar as they have control) feel that way precisely because they believe it is rude for anyone to take that risk. They might even object to the inclusion of examples of taboo terms in a scholarly discussion or book, like the present one.

Certainly, however, speakers don't all react in a single way to all taboo terms. Many of us consider the overall context in which a given taboo term is uttered and react in a way appropriate to that context, particularly if the taboo term involves things common to all people (rather than discriminating against only certain groups of people), such as bodily effluent, genitalia, or sexual activity (as opposed to sexual orientation). If an adult says, "Shit," when talking casually at a barbecue and then a few moments later a three-year-old child, for example, drops his hotdog and says with dismay, "Shit," clearly echoing the adult, some people would even laugh. (This is not to say that the very people who laughed wouldn't then immediately explain to the child that such terms aren't to be used in polite society. That is, you might laugh even if you are someone who censors your own and your children's language.) There are also many people who use lots of taboo terms in casual language with friends, where the very sprinkling of one's language with these terms is a mark of the strength of the friendship. Those same speakers might be surprised or even offended if a stranger came up and out of the blue started speaking in that manner. Context definitely matters for these speakers.

Nevertheless, taboo terms always have the potential to evoke strong emotional reactions, which means they are great potential tools for manipulation. We're all aware of the use of taboo terms to incite people to action (perhaps to initiate a fight or to march in a protest or many other things) or to keep people from acting (perhaps demoralizing or belittling them into submission). Here I'll point out two quite different types of manipulation and leave it to you to recognize others around you.

My coauthor and I work in a rather elite small liberal arts college. When people find out where we work, sometimes they can feel a little intimidated. They'll say things like, "Boy, you sure must be a brain to teach all those brainy kids." My coauthor sometimes adopts extremely casual language in such situations in the hopes of putting the people at ease and helping them not to think of her as a snob. For example, she was having a construction crew put in a tall bamboo fence at her house, and when they asked what it was like teaching at "the great Swarthmore," she said, "Generally, it's wonderful, but now and then it's hell, you know." She took a risk. The guys might have thought she was being phony and patronizing them (which she wasn't—she curses like a sailor). They might have been people who find taboo terms offensive and never use them. Either result would have been a pity. However, her hope was that they'd feel more comfortable with her—and not hesitate to come in to use the bathroom, get themselves a drink, or whatever. It was an attempt to manipulate—to make herself seem like one of them. Often when we try to fit into or relate in a friendly way to a new group we will use whatever language we believe is typical of that group—which sometimes might include taboo terms.

This example is quite straightforward, and the construction crew was probably aware of what my coauthor was trying to do. However, more subtle forms of manipulation with taboo terms occur all the time. This one involves a third Swarthmore professor, whom we'll call Professor B. Professor B has the habit of showing up in a class of primarily first-year students on the first day of the first semester of their college experience dressed in jeans and liberally dropping taboo terms and up-to-date teen language throughout his lecture. What is he hoping to do? We guess that he's using a kind of "shock and awe" approach. He's giving conflicting information, playing mind games with the students. On the one hand, he is the professor—he's the one at the lectern, and he's the old guy. On the other hand, he's just an ordinary guy (witness the jeans) who happens to be hip (witness the taboo terms and the most recent teen jargon), and he's inviting you (via his clothing and language) to speak to him just as you would to anyone else. He's sending a message: *Stay in this class, and you'll be shocked and awed throughout the term 'cause I'm exciting, and I know how to reach you, and you can always reach me.* Is he effective? He's one of the more popular professors on campus (though neither my coauthor nor I feel comfortable at all with this kind of manipulation).

Summing up our exploration of language and power, I've presented a number of different scenarios in which utterances (or certain words within larger utterances) come with a level of meaning that can be extremely powerful without being immediately obvious to people. A presupposition is an entailment of an utterance that is silently taken for granted (i.e., not asserted as something that is at issue and open to discussion) and must be true in order for the utterance to be meaningful in a nonmanipulative way. A conversational implicature may seem like an entailment, which logically follows from an utterance, but it is not. It is just an implication that can be canceled. It can therefore be used to send a powerful message without a strong commitment on the part of the speaker (or writer). Framing allows speakers to evoke powerful thoughts in people's heads without giving them a choice in the matter. Finally, as for taboo terms, everybody knows how powerful their effect can be in certain obvious contexts, but they can be used to manipulate more subtly as well.

Further Reading

Allan, K., and K. Burridge. 1991. *Euphemism and dysphemism: Language used as shield and weapon.* New York: Oxford University Press.

Andersson, L., and P. Trudgill. 1990. *Bad language.* Oxford: Blackwell.

Beaver, D. 1997. Presupposition. In J. van Benthem and A. ter Meulen, eds., *The handbook of logic and language,* 939–1008. Cambridge, Mass.: Elsevier/MIT Press.

Bolinger, D. 1980. *Language, the loaded weapon: The use and abuse of language today.* New York: Longman.

Grice, H. P. 1975. Logic and conversation. In P. Cole and J. Morgan, eds., *Syntax and semantics.* Vol. 3, *Speech acts,* 41–58. New York:

Academic Press. Reprinted in H. P. Grice, ed., *Studies in the way of words*, 22–40. Cambridge, Mass.: Harvard University Press, 1989.

Lakoff, G. 2004. *Don't think of an elephant: Know your values and frame the debate: The essential guide for progressives.* White River Junction, Vt.: Chelsea Green.

———. 2006. *Whose freedom? The battle over America's most important idea.* New York: Ferrar, Straus, and Giroux.

McEnery, T. 2006. *Swearing in English: Bad language, purity, and power from 1586 to the present.* London: Routledge.

Shuy, R. W. 2005. *Creative language crimes: How law enforcement uses (and misuses) language.* New York: Oxford University Press.

Keywords

language and power
language of advertising
language politics

14 Does exposure to and use of offensive language harm children?

Many people believe that exposure to offensive language harms children but that censorship of children's language and literature does not. Because such censorship is on the rise in the United States, it's timely to consider its effects. In addition, because so many truly thoughtful people are in favor of censorship, I believe it is my responsibility to present the other side of the debate.

Censorship of language is often an attempt to control language change. When I was a child, for example, many words having to do with sexual reproduction were taboo; teachers would scold children (or do worse) for using them. The list of words I was not allowed to say included names of body parts such as *penis* and *vagina*, words that are used in classrooms today. (Many of these words have since lost their nasty connotations.) Efforts to censor language, for reasons of religion, political correctness, or anything else, aim to control language change by putting certain words out of use. Censorship is definitely a linguistic matter.

I am particularly interested in this issue, however, because, as well as being a linguist, I am a fiction writer for children. In addition, I teach writing workshops to children and adults in schools and writing associations all over the United States and many places abroad. As a writer, the two biggest language misconceptions I deal with are these:

1. Some language is correct, but other language isn't—so the character in my book shouldn't say, "I swim good," but, instead, "I swim well."
2. Some language is dangerous and doesn't belong in children's books, especially not coming out of children's mouths.

The first type of comment often comes from editors, sometimes otherwise brilliant editors. Typically, I cringe. To understand my reaction, read chapter 8. "I swim good" is perfectly grammatical for many speakers. It is the product of a grammar that allows adjectives to modify verbs and verb phrases. That same grammar produces sentences such as "She works hard," which probably most native speakers of English can produce in their ordinary speech. That "I swim well" is also grammatical (though stilted for many) does not in any way call into question the grammaticality of "I swim good"; grammars generate an infinite number of sentences and multiple sentence types. In the speech of a very few people, only adverbs can modify verbs and verb phrases (so they would not say, "She works hard"). For many other people, though (indeed, for most Americans), adverbs and some adjectives can modify verbs and verb phrases (although people differ on the range of adjectives they allow). For still many others, adjectives more typically than adverbs can modify verbs and verb phrases (so they would prefer "They learn quick" to "They learn quickly"). Younger speakers are more predominant in the third group, a fact that suggests that this is the present direction of language change regarding the modification of verbs and verb phrases.

By far the harder misconception to fight, however, is the second—censorship. What follows is a position statement against censorship, which relies in part on your having read earlier chapters in this book. It has the following form:

1. Language is a basic human need and, therefore, a basic human right. It's like eating or breathing. That right must be protected from censorship.

2. Language does not equal thought, so attempts to censor thought by censoring language are both misguided and bound to fail. Furthermore, if language does equal thought, attempts to censor thought are disrespectful of the humanity of children. So if I were wrong, and these attempts were not futile, they'd be vile in any case.

3. Language is a fundamental way of organizing the expression of our experiences, both external and internal. It is a way to give legitimacy to the spirit. It is, therefore, a creative faculty, an artistic ability, and as such it should not be censored. Furthermore, talking and writing don't cost money, so they are artistic outlets available to every level of society, including the most powerless—our children. For this reason alone, the creative faculty of language should be even more vigilantly protected.

Many of the chapters in this book give relevant arguments for the first point. I want to add that I support this right even when it comes to something as hideous as hate speech. Of course, hate speech that is likely to incite imminent criminal acts is itself criminal and cannot be tolerated. However, that's quite different from hate speech that is a simple statement of opinion. Indeed, it's the right to express opinions that the majority do not agree with—unpopular positions—that we must work the hardest to protect since all of us have the right not to listen if we choose.

Chapter 4 gives relevant arguments for the second point.

It is the third point that we have not yet addressed in any way. We need to look at the forces on both sides of the censorship line and the values of the art of literature. The misconception I hope to debunk is that use of or exposure to so-called offensive language or literature is harmful to children.

I begin by presenting the area I expect the most resistance to: my ideas about children's language use. Many people take offense at various types of language, depending on sociological and personal factors. I take offense at language that smacks of social elitism, but I am rarely offended by swearing. My mother took offense at both. My youngest son takes offense at neither. I don't object to people being offended by certain language, but sometimes adults forbid children from using such language—even adults who use that language themselves—on the grounds that using it is harmful to children.

This is objectionable not (only) because it is hypocritical (though that is certainly objectionable in itself) but because, I believe, it is incorrect. Children have all kinds of thoughts and feelings, and we, as adults who care about them, need to know what they are thinking if they want to tell us. If we object to how children express themselves, they might not talk about some matters at all, which would be truly harmful indeed.

However, even if children accept our language censorship guidelines, they might be thinking precisely the offensive thought behind the word. That is, by controlling the word, it does not follow that we control the thought. Often adults offer children alternative words, veering them away from *damn* and toward *darn* or perhaps some idiosyncratically chosen or coined word. Nonetheless, those youngsters who say *blinkity* to everyone they're angry at and who stamp their feet and wish vile things would happen to their younger siblings may, in fact, have cruder and more violent thoughts than those who say *asshole* when they lift their defiant little chin to their father. If you truly believe that saying *damn* harms children, how can you not believe that saying *darn* or *blinkity* harms them? This sort of censorship is out of focus. It's as absurd as concluding that children are well behaved and happy because they're wearing attractive, clean clothes. We should encourage our children to express their thoughts and feelings to us in whatever ways are natural to them if we want to help them through the growing-up process.

Let's now turn to the issue of censorship in literature. Let me give you some telling facts about how important this question is to the American public:

- The November/December 2000 bulletin of the Society of Children's Book Writers and Illustrators included an article titled "Banned Books: The Case for Getting Involved."
- The fall 2000 bulletin of the Authors Guild included the articles "Know It When You See It? You Can Still See It on the Internet" and "Celebrate Banned Books."
- Volume 33, no. 3 (December 2000) of the journal of the Associated Writing Programs (AWP) included *The Writer's Chronicle*, "Self-censorship and the Alternatives."

I subscribe to all three publications. In the fall of 2000 I was preparing for a presentation on censorship for the winter meeting of the Linguistic Society of America. Given these publications, I didn't have to leave my home at all to do my research; instead, the research bombarded me. Censorship is a major battle, and it is being fought right now.

I was a speaker at the annual meeting of the National Council of Teachers of English (NCTE) in November 2000, and I received a copy of their publication, the *ALAN Review* 27(3) (spring/summer 2000), which included two relevant articles: "Creating a

Censorship Simulation" and "Middle Schoolers and the Right to Read." Professor Robert Small of Radford University in Virginia was cited in both articles. I wrote to him, and he sent me a thick packet of articles on censorship, as well as the *ALAN Review* 20(2) (1993), which is entirely devoted to censorship.

I learned from these materials that the number of censorship episodes chronicled by the People for the American Way (PFAW, Norman Lear's nonprofit activist organization) was seven times greater in 1996–1997 than it was in 1988–1989, the numbers increasing each year. The PFAW discontinued publication of this valuable yearly record, so I do not know what has happened since—but I'm not sanguine. In 1999–2000, 152 challenges to books were filed in Texas schools alone (Texas is the most frequent site of such challenges), and forty-two banning incidents resulted (catalogued in the report of the American Civil Liberties Union of Texas, September 2000). In these censorship proceedings, the dozen top complaints about books were the following:

1. offensive language, the most cited complaint (24 percent)
2. explicit sexual descriptions, the next most cited complaint (23 percent)
3. incidents of violence or brutality, including rape (13 percent)
4. disparagement of family values (8 percent)
5. treatment of satanism, the occult, or witchcraft (8 percent)
6. "new age," antireligious stories (7 percent)
7. examples of racism (5 percent)
8. examples of substance abuse (4 percent)
9. materials that include depressing, morbid topics (3 percent)
10. attacks on patriotism or established authority (2.75 percent)

11. texts that include antifeminism or sexism (1 percent)
12. derogatory images of handicapped people (0.47 percent)

When a book is challenged, an imposing and growing number of school principals and superintendents around the country cave in by taking it out of the libraries. The biggest targets are elementary schools, whose children are least likely to be able to get to a public library on their own, so the censorship is most effective and destructive here.

When a book is removed from a library, editors in publishing houses notice. As they work on the manuscripts in progress, they ask authors to make revisions less for artistic reasons than to avoid controversy. What winds up in the child's hands is sanitized.

Worse, the marketing division of the publishing house is alarmed, so publishing houses self-censor to the point of not taking a chance on a book that has literary merit. (See the AWP article mentioned earlier.) Unpublished works are lost forever.

Worse still, creative writing teachers often warn their students about censorship and sometimes even censor their students' work themselves. Joyce Greenberg Lott writes about this dilemma from the point of view of a successful writing teacher in the *Writer's Chronicle* 33(4) (February 2001). Most horrible of all, writers listen. When a book like *Snow Falling on Cedars* is banned, writers recoil and put projects on ice.

The problem is so big that there is a National Coalition against Censorship, formed in the 1990s, which produces the quarterly *Censorship News*. The American Library Association (ALA) has an Intellectual Freedom Committee, which publishes the bimonthly *Newsletter on Intellectual Freedom* and sponsors an annual Banned Books Week, in which everyone is urged to check out one of the books on the list of one hundred books most often banned. The ALA publishes this list. The NCTE has a Standing Committee against Censorship, which publishes a pamphlet titled "The Students' Right to Read," and its major periodicals often dedicate issues to censorship. The International Reading Association (IRA) has a Committee on Intellectual Freedom and, with NCTE, produced the anticensorship pamphlet "Common Ground." There is a Freedom to Read Foundation and the People for the American Way (mentioned earlier), so the anticensorship groups are gathering forces.

It is not clear, however, whether they can hold their ground. The foes are multiple and powerful and include the Christian Coalition, the Family Research Council, the Eagle Forum, and many others. Support from such groups led to the Communications Decency Act (CDA), which was passed in 1996, some portions of which were ruled unconstitutional by the U.S. Supreme Court. Immediately after the Supreme Court ruled against the CDA, Congress passed the Child Online Privacy Protection Act (COPPA), which requires Internet publishers to ensure that minors are barred from accessing material deemed to be "harmful" to them according to "contemporary community standards." Because Web publishers are unable to restrict access to their pages by geographical locale, COPPA effectively forces them to abide by the standards of the most restrictive and conservative communities in the country. Furthermore, people who use these filters have no way of knowing exactly what pages will be blocked.

In a study conducted in 2000, a thousand randomly chosen website addresses in the dot-com domain were submitted to the SurfWatch filter. Of the sites this filter blocked as sexually explicit, a team of evaluators found four out of five misclassified. The filter blocked the sites of a storage company in California, a limousine service in Maryland, and an antiques dealer in Wales. In another study that year, the first fifty URLs in the dot-edu domain that were blocked by Symantec Corporation's I-Gear filter included at least three out of four sites that had nothing to do with sex. One in Portuguese was about a milk pasteurization system, one consisted of sections from Edward Gibbon's *Decline and Fall of the Roman Empire*, and one was a passage in Latin from the *Confessions* of Saint Augustine (probably triggered by the presence of the Latin preposition *cum*, which means 'with'). So the whole Internet filter proposal is a farce. However, even if the technology could perform flawlessly, this sort of censorship is as problematic as any other. Moreover, systems deny access to adults who either lack verification credentials (such as credit cards) or don't want to identify themselves on the Internet. Other acts of censorship follow quickly in such a climate. The New York Regents Exam, for example, was criticized by free speech groups in 2002 for altering literacy passages in their reading exams to make them more politically correct (substituting *heck* for *hell* and the like). In sum, there are multiple efforts for censorship on multiple fronts, and the zeal behind them is so great that their clear harm is hardly noticed.

Most attempts to censor children's literature—in books or on the Internet—are, I believe, well intended. They are not meant to harm. Rather, they grow out of concern for children's well-being and the desire to control the world that children encounter in ways that their supporters believe are beneficial—although there is little evidence that censorship does that. There is, however, reason to believe that censorship harms children by denying them their basic rights, just as much as it denies rights to adults.

One of the most powerful examples of this kind of harm is a book that was banned in the second half of the twentieth century—Harper

Lee's *To Kill a Mockingbird*—because of an interracial romance. Many people who support the censorship of books today would never include this book on a to-be-banned list. They would not want to be associated with that kind of racism. They would not want to teach their children that an interracial romance is wrong. Our societal values change, and what once seemed offensive may later be seen as a right we want to protect.

Let's consider three types of subject matter that censorship efforts often target and learn how such suppression can harm children.

First, representations of a harsh world in which unpleasant things happen are often the target of censors, but children may actually need to encounter such accounts. The *Censorship News* in the fall of 2000 said, "Angry weird songs often make adolescents feel less lonely and more connected to other kids." I believe from my personal experience and observation that the same is true of stories. Many of us do not express our wickedest thoughts or our most horrendous fears, which we, as adults, know are common. We know this partly from living so long and, for some of us, partly from reading. Reading gives us access to the characters' innermost thoughts and allows an intimacy that is often rare in real life. As I read Jane Hamilton's *Map of the World* I was grateful to see my fears and paranoias come to life, and I remember this gratitude when I write for children. No one is lonelier than youngsters who believe their thoughts are wickeder than everyone else's. Children don't have years of life experience to draw on when trying to put their thoughts and fears in perspective. They need to read about characters who have all the problems they worry about, and children do worry—middle-class, pampered, and protected children, as well as starving children in war-ravaged lands. They need to read about "depressing, morbid topics" (number 9 on the list of reasons for banning books) if only to be able to dispel their power.

Robert Cormier, the author of *The Chocolate War, I Am the Cheese*, and so many other excruciating books for young adults, said, "It is possible to be a peaceful man, to abhor violence, to love children and flowers and old Beatles songs, and still be aware of the contusions and abrasions this world inflicts on us. Not to write happy endings doesn't mean the writer doesn't believe in them. Literature should penetrate all the chambers of the human heart, even the dark ones" (quoted in Anita Silvey, *Children's Books and Their Creators*, page 105). Richard Peck, a winner of the highest prize that can be bestowed on children's books, the Newbery, at the August 2001 annual meeting of the Society of Children's Book Writers and Illustrators said, "Writers for children cannot afford to traffic in happy endings, because if we do, we risk leaving our readers defenseless."

Second, sexually explicit material is a target of censors, although again there is much evidence that children need to read such material. Sexually transmitted viruses and diseases, including HIV/AIDS, are increasing among the young in the United States, and unwanted pregnancies occur more often here than in other industrialized countries, where comprehensive sex education is more readily available (see *Censorship News*—the newsletter of the National Coalition against Censorship). Ignorance is a major culprit. Keeping sex out of children's reading contributes to ignorance and thus to the rise of these diseases and pregnancies. Sex is almost invariably a controversial matter in children's literature because it is a controversial matter in our society. However, as Nancy Garden, author of the prize-winning and popular book about a lesbian teen, *Annie on My Mind*, said at the November 2001 meeting of the Michigan Library Association, "If you remove what's controversial from the bookshelves, there isn't a lot left."

Third, violence is a target of censors, and often this type of censorship is justified on the grounds that exposure to representations of violence contributes to violent behavior. However, in September 2000, Senator John McCain, chair of the Senate Commerce Committee, led hearings about the effects of the entertainment industry on children's welfare, hearings in response to a Federal Trade Commission's report earlier that month. McCain said, "Scholars and observers generally have agreed that exposure to violence in entertainment media alone does not cause a child to commit a violent act and that it is not the sole, or even necessarily the most important factor contributing to youth aggression, antisocial attitudes and violence." Richard Rhodes, author of *Why They Kill*, wrote in the *New York Times* on September 17, 2000, that "violence isn't learned from mock violence. There is good evidence—causal evidence, not correlational—that it's learned in personal violent encounters, beginning with the brutalization of children by their parents or peers.... Violence is on the decline in America, but if we want to reduce it even further, protecting children from real violence in their lives... is the place to begin."

What should we conclude? If I argue against censors by saying that reading a curse word cannot influence a child to curse or that reading material that questions the existence of a god cannot influence a child also to question that existence, I'm essentially claiming that the written word has little power. But the written word has tremendous power: What we read can open worlds. The very purpose of good literature is to disturb, to make us take a second look at previously held assumptions, to make us take a first look at things we haven't encountered. As a writer, I would stop writing if I didn't think my words disturbed.

My point, though, is that, if we keep a child from reading a curse word, we are in no way guaranteed that the child will not think exactly that curse, and there's certainly no evidence that teens who don't read have less sex than teens who do. However, what we can be assured of is that the child who is deprived of reading a scene through to its end; who is deprived of hearing the ring of real discourse in moments of terror, desperation, anger, or indeed love and joy; and who is deprived of experiencing the thrills that the protagonists of stories feel—that is, the child who can read only censored material—loses the emotional insights and the truth of the story.

Tim O'Brien, the author of the magnificent novel *The Things They Carried*, says, "You can tell a true war story if it embarrasses you. If you don't care for obscenity, you don't care for the truth; if you don't care for the truth, watch how you vote. Send guys to war, they come home talking dirty."

There's no way around it: The cost of censorship is truth. When we censor the material available to our children, we lie to them, and lies to children are unforgivable. It's our job, yours and mine—as people who know that language does not equal thought and who recognize the values of language—to join the battle and disabuse our neighbors of their misconceptions about what censorship will and will not accomplish.

Works Cited

Brown, J., and E. Stephens, eds. 2000. Creating a censorship simulation. *ALAN Review* 27(3): 27–30.

Celebrate banned books. 2000, Fall. *Authors Guild Bulletin*, 49.

Censorship News. 2000, Fall. National Coalition against Censorship Newsletter 79.

Chen, A. 2000, Fall. Know it when you see it? You can still see it on the Internet. *Authors Guild Bulletin*, 11.

Cormier, R. 1977. *I am the cheese*. New York: Laureleaf.

————. 1991. *The chocolate war*. New York: Laureleaf.

Fore, A. 2002, Summer. N.Y. Regents Exam examined. *Authors Guild Bulletin*, 65, 39.

Garden, Nancy. 1982. *Annie on my mind*. New York: Farrar, Straus, Giroux.

Greenberg Lott, J. 2001, February. The yin and yang of teaching creative writing. *Writer's Chronicle* 33(4): 40–44.

Guterson, D. 1995. *Snow falling on cedars*. New York: Vintage.

Hamilton, J. 1999. *A map of the world*. New York: Anchor.

Krishnaswami, U. 2000, November–December. Banned books: The case for getting involved. *Society of Children's Book Writers and Illustrators Bulletin*, 9.

Lee, Harper. 1995. *To kill a mockingbird*. New York: HarperCollins.

O'Brien, T. 1999. *The things they carried*, 69. New York: Broadway.

Rhodes, R. 2000. *Why they kill*. New York: Vintage.

Schiffrin, A. 2000. Self-censorship and the alternatives: The self-censorship of big publishers and their money. *Writer's Chronicle* 33(3): 50–56.

Silvey, A. 1995. *Children's books and their creators*. Boston: Houghton Mifflin.

Simmons, J. 2000. Middle schoolers and the right to read. *ALAN Review* 27(3): 45–49.

Further Reading

Brown, J. 1994. *Preserving intellectual freedom: Fighting censorship in our schools*. Urbana, Ill.: National Council of Teachers of English.

Davis, J., ed. 1979. *Dealing with censorship*. Urbana, Ill.: National Council of Teachers of English.

Journal of Youth Services in Libraries 13(2) (2000, Winter). Association for Library Service to Children.

Karolides, N., L. Burress, and J. Kean, eds. 1993. *Censored books: Critical viewpoints*. Metuchen, N.J.: Scarecrow.

Keywords

banned books
censorship
taboo language and children

15

What do we lose when a language dies? And who cares?

Linguists predict that, of the human languages that are currently spoken worldwide—approximately seven thousand—only about half will still be spoken by the end of this century. You may ask why we should be concerned about this and say it's simply a fact of life that languages die out. If there aren't enough speakers who feel they need to use a language, then perhaps it's meant to go extinct, and we're better off without it. Isn't it better if more people around the world speak fewer languages, ones spoken by big populations (which I'll label "big" languages, as opposed to languages spoken by small populations, which I'll label "small" languages), so that there aren't as many language barriers to impede global communication?

There are a number of reasons that the answer to this question is no and that this line of reasoning is not on the right track. As the following discussion of three of these reasons explains, we are in fact better off with those small languages or at least with having recorded them before they become extinct.

One reason, which I personally feel strongly about in my role as a mother bringing up her children bilingually, is that a language is not just one of the many arbitrary ways in which a group of people happens to communicate. Rather, languages encode whole culture and belief systems.

When I hear other bilingual families talk about how their kids reach a certain age and then refuse to speak the minority language,

I get very worried that the same might happen to my son Niko. Being surrounded by the language everyone speaks at school—in this case, English—the language spoken by the parents at home suddenly seems outdated, unnecessary, worthless even. Of course, I want Niko to have native proficiency in English, the language spoken in the country he is growing up in, but I also want him to maintain his other native language, his true mother tongue. I've been living in the United States for fifteen years now and feel completely comfortable expressing myself in English both at home with my American husband and at work with my students and colleagues. Yet, in certain situations I automatically switch to German, my native language. When I have a lot of counting or calculations to do, for example, I whisper the numbers to myself in German. The same holds for the months of the year and the alphabet. Basic vocabulary like this seems to be so deeply ingrained that it's easier to access in one's native language than in the second language, regardless of how long the second language has been dominant in one's life. The mother tongue is also the dominant language when it comes to interactions with babies or cute little animals. The high-pitched, slow, and often exaggerated speech many of us affectionately use with babies is called "motherese" for a reason.

Knowing that Niko will probably not fall back on German as his default like I do somehow hurts. Sharing a language means not only knowing the same vocabulary and grammar rules but also sharing certain ways of expressing our understanding of the world. Indeed, humor in one language often differs enormously from that in another language—so much so that translated jokes often fall flat. I love it when Niko, who is two and a half as I'm writing this chapter, engages in silly little German word games with me, for example. This is a kind of humor that's very language specific and can't be translated. At this point in our lives, Niko's German grandparents are still very much involved in his life, and when they come to visit, it's beautiful to see how Niko's German gets reinforced. It's crucial for him to have people around him other than me who communicate with him in German.

But again, unfortunately it's only natural for children—especially for those whose parents' native language is not only rare in their immediate environment but, unlike German, is spoken by only a handful of elderly people in the world—to hit a phase where the majority language seems so much more essential to them that they rebel against the minority language. They learn very early on that, in order to get ahead in life, avoid being an outcast, and instead belong to the in-group, they need the majority language. Any other language is perceived as more of a burden or an embarrassment than a connection to a valuable culture and belief system.

Examples of very small languages that are on the verge of extinction or are already extinct are Tofa in Siberia, which has about thirty speakers left, Vilela in Argentina, which has only two speakers left, and Makah in Washington State, which has no more native speakers left, only speakers with partial knowledge and a few second language learners. Of course, the situation of children growing up in a family speaking an endangered language like Tofa or Vilela and facing the pressure of having to conform to the majority language, Russian or Spanish, respectively, is much more urgent than that of German-English bilingual children like my son. When children refuse to maintain an endangered language, they have brought the language one step closer to extinction, whereas children who refuse to speak a language like German because it's not the majority language spoken in the country they live in only make their families sad. Still, from the perspective of the child in either situation, the motivation is probably the same: a human being's natural striving for conformity, efficiency, and opportunity.

A second reason to preserve endangered languages as long as possible, at least until they have been documented (which I also have a personal connection to, this time in my role as a linguist), is that any language, no matter how small, gives us insight into how the human mind organizes information and, in particular, how it structures language. If the theories linguists posit are based merely on the 83 biggest languages spoken by 80 percent of the global population, not taking into account the other 6,917 spoken by the other 20 percent of the people (in fact, 3,500 languages are spoken by only 0.2 percent of people worldwide), then rare but nonetheless possible linguistic structures (sound patterns, word formations, word order possibilities in sentences, ways of organizing information about the world into lexical items, and so on) are surely being missed. Chances are that these rare linguistic structures, if discovered, disprove some of the seemingly well-established theoretical assumptions.

When it comes to word order typology, for example, the order subject-verb-object (SVO), as in English and Italian, and the order SOV, as in Japanese and Turkish, are very commonly found. Not quite as common but by now unsurprising to linguists are the orders VSO (as in Irish) and VOS (as in the Austronesian language Malagasy). Languages that put the object first, however, are extremely rare and would be unheard of if it weren't for research on endangered languages. Urarina, spoken by fewer than three thousand people in the Amazon jungle of Peru, for example, has OVS order and therefore provides counterevidence to theories that don't allow for the derivation of an object-first language.

An example of language structuring that might be easier to relate to is number systems. For example, if you are a speaker of English and you count up to high numbers, how does English make you organize and express the numbers? You never have to count higher than 10 before you recycle number terms. We have ten words for the numbers 1 through 10, and when we continue, with the exception of 11 (*eleven*) and 12 (*twelve*), we simply use the number 10 and add one of our nine single-digit numbers to it: 3+10 (***thir**-teen*), 4+10, (***four**-teen*), 5+10 (***fif**-teen*), and so on. The words for 20, 30, 40, and so on are also based on our single-digit numbers (***twen**-ty*, ***thir**-ty*, ***for**-ty*, etc.), and for the numbers in between, we again add numbers from 1 to 9: 20+1 (*twenty-**one***), 20+2 (*twenty-**two***), 20+3 (*twenty-**three***), and so on. This is why we say the English number system is a decimal or base 10 system. If you speak French, you've probably noticed that counting works differently than in English when you get up to 70, 80, and 90. Instead of there being a word for 70 that is based on the French word for 7, 70 is expressed as 60+10 (*soixante-dix*). Then, when it comes to 80, the French switch to a base 20 system, so the word for 80 is 4×20 (*quatre-vingt*), and this then is the new base for 90, which is expressed as 4×20+10 (*quatre-vingt-dix*).

In the documentary *The Linguists*, my Swarthmore colleague David Harrison and his research partner Greg Anderson are shown eliciting data from a speaker of a language, Sora, spoken in India, which has a combined base 12 and base 20 system, so that the number 93 is expressed as 4×20+12+1. This is a way of chunking numbers we never would have thought possible if it weren't for research on small, endangered languages. The point is that different languages have a variety of ways of structuring the knowledge that makes up our linguistic competence, and this shows us how the human mind can operate. Our own language often puts blinders on us in terms of how we think people can organize information, so we rely on anthropological linguistics (including research on endangered languages) to venture beyond our preconceptions.

One may argue that small languages shouldn't be the focus of investigation because it's virtually impossible to get a large enough database to draw reliable conclusions from. Carefully conducted research involving even a single speaker, however, can be the start of a line of inquiry that leads to crucial new insights into human cognition. We just have to make the effort to find a starting point. Every little bit of new information then serves to further establish or redirect the initial findings.

The third reason is probably the most compelling because it concerns an issue that is of interest to all of us, whether or not we're raising our children bilingually and whether or not we happen to be linguists. It's the fact that language death goes hand in hand with the erosion of our human knowledge base. As David Harrison convincingly puts it, "Most of what humans have learned over the millennia about how to thrive on this planet is encapsulated in threatened languages. If we let them slip away, we may compromise our very ability to survive as our ballooning population strains earth's ecosystems" (2007, 19).

How exactly does language encapsulate people's vital knowledge? Although any thought or concept can certainly be expressed in any language (see chapter 4), we know from trying to translate one language into another that different languages may use very different strategies of encoding information (see chapter 3).

In so-called synthetic or inflectional languages, grammatical information like person and number, tense, and case (markers for subject, direct object, indirect object, etc.) are expressed as affixes, that is, as parts of words. In so-called analytic or isolating languages, this kind of grammatical information is expressed in the form of separate words. What a speaker of German can express in three words, as in the following sentence, takes six words in Mandarin Chinese, for example:

Wir spielten Klavier   [German]
we played piano
wo men tan gang qin le [Mandarin Chinese, tones omitted]
I plural play piano instrument completed

The information of first-person plural is delivered in German with a single word, the pronoun *wir* but in Mandarin with the first-person pronoun *wo* plus the plural marker *men*. The information of the past tense of the verb meaning 'play' is delivered in German with the single word *spielten*, where *-t-* is the past tense affix, but in Mandarin with the uninflected form of the verb *tan* and the completed action marker *le*.

Grammatical information, of course, is not knowledge that's vital to the survival of humankind. It's part of our mental grammar, and we acquire it subconsciously as young children (see chapter 1). I mention it here because, just as pieces of grammatical information can either be combined with a stem into a single word or be expressed as separate words, several pieces of lexical (not purely grammatical but contentful) information can be conveyed as either a single word or many words making up a whole sentence. In Todzhu, a language that is mutually comprehensible with Tofa, spoken in the Sayan Mountains of southern Siberia, single words for certain reindeer correspond to an entire sentence, if not more, in English. The concept of 'male domesticated reindeer from second fall to third fall; first mating season; may be castrated or not, but even if not, will probably not be allowed to mate,' for example, is expressed simply as the word *döngür*. The word for 'female domesticated reindeer in her first autumn of mating' is *myndyzhak*. The Todzhu people are reindeer herders and hunters, camping in tents year-round. It makes sense, then, that they have efficient ways of classifying different kinds of reindeer. Their language, including their reindeer names, that is, the way in which they package information into words, encodes crucial information about their way of life and their survival strategies in the rough terrain of the Siberian mountains. One could learn about these people's way of life and survival strategies simply from observing their behavior, but documenting their language is much more efficient. Just knowing a few names for reindeer, we gain an insight into what physical attributes and other characteristics of reindeer are important for herding them effectively. Most of this kind of knowledge cannot be found in any textbook or database. Since the languages spoken by indigenous people often do not have a writing system, the knowledge they encode about their speakers' natural habitat is transmitted strictly orally from generation to generation. If a new generation comes to believe that the older generation's language is useless in the modern world, the days of the language, and thus the vital indigenous knowledge it so efficiently encodes, are numbered.

Since reindeer are not a high priority for most of us, let me bring up an example of information packaging that hits closer to home. Consider the English kinship term *uncle*. When we want to distinguish between an uncle on the mother's side and one on the father's side, we need to say *mother's brother* versus *father's brother*. Or, if we mean the in-laws, we have to say *mother's sister's husband* versus *father's sister's husband*. While we can in fact make these distinctions between the various types of uncle, we don't need to very often, and that's a good thing because the English language doesn't allow us to in a particularly efficient manner. The situation is different for speakers of Tofa. There's no general word for 'uncle.'

Each of the aforementioned types of uncle has its own label, and this is because kinship relations play a socially important role. Just as it is necessary for a Tofa reindeer hunter to have one-word labels for the many different types of reindeer he needs to be able to tell apart, it is vitally important for a member of a Tofa family to have a convenient labeling system for the family's intricate kinship relations.

You may have heard the claim that Eskimo has many words for snow. Before I talk about this claim, I want to point out that the term *Eskimo* is taken as a racial slur by some of the people it is intended to subsume; however, since the term is a language-family name and covers a variety of languages for which there is no other cover term (including Yupik and Inuktitut), I use it here.

Two things concerning the claim that Eskimo has many words for snow are false, but one is true and very much relevant to the questions addressed in this chapter.

It's false that the Eskimo languages have all that many more words for snow than other languages do (although it is true, as I'll explain in a moment, that Yupik has an impressive number of different words for ice). Can you think of some English words that describe variants of snow? *Flurry, powder, hail, sleet, slush*...I'm sure you can extend this list, especially if you live in an area that gets a lot of snow or if you regularly do winter sports like skiing and snowboarding.

It's also false that the various words for snow in each of the Eskimo languages show that the speakers understand differentiations in snow types that are beyond the comprehension of speakers of other languages. As explained in chapter 4, whether a language has a one-word label or needs a whole sentence to express a concept, its speakers are equally capable of grasping the concept. A language that lacks a one-word label simply doesn't allow its speakers to integrate the concept into everyday conversation as efficiently.

This leads me to the part of the claim about the Eskimo words for snow that is true. It certainly is true that, even if the Eskimo languages have only a few more snow words than we do, this fact is linguistically interesting and significant. While it's simply common sense that anyone who regularly deals with freezing temperatures probably uses more snow-related terminology than people who live in warmer climates, most of these snow-savvy people are not speakers of an endangered language, living in an ecosystem in a part of the world that mainstream society knows virtually nothing about. The knowledge encoded in the Eskimo words for snow and the way these words package information give linguists important insights into the various Eskimo cultures and way of life, including survival strategies.

To conclude this excursion to the Eskimo languages, I want to point out (as promised earlier) that Yupik, while it may not have a particularly large number of words for snow, does have a huge number of words for sea ice, ninety-nine different labels to be exact. To give you a little taste of this wealth of vocabulary, here are the definitions of three of the ninety-nine words, taken from a book written in part by two native speakers of Yupik:

> Alqimiin: Overhanging snow on the edge of ice; dangerous spot. Ice formed from pressured snow, usually by snow banks, cliffs, or at the ice edge. It is thin or hollow with no bottom, and it is usually sticking out, easy to fall off. It is very dangerous to walk on. If you step on it, you may fall through into the water.
>
> Maklukestaq: Solid ice that has no pressure ridges. This ice is kind of smooth and also a little bumpy. When you are

pulling a boat on this ice, the boat even moves on the
bumps a little. Best to work on.

Nunaavalleq: Any form of ice floe that walrus have stayed
on for a long period of time. If the walrus have stayed
on the ice for five days or more, the ice will look dark
(dirty) from their bodily waste.

From these definitions we get an idea of how much vital cultural
knowledge is contained in the different words the Yupik have
for sea ice. Using the appropriate labels when talking about sea
ice with a friend or coworker efficiently communicates to them
whether the ice is safe to step and work on, for example.

In order to convince even the most skeptical reader of how
important it is to preserve or at least record and learn from small
languages, I'm ending this chapter with another quote from my
colleague David Harrison, author of *When Languages Die*:

> Societies that rely on nature for survival have
> developed technologies to cultivate, domesticate, and
> exploit... resources [such as medicinal plants, fish, reindeer,
> moon phases, wind patterns, and rice plants]. The fact that
> we now have modern farming, laboratories, calendars, and
> libraries does not render traditional knowledge obsolete.
> If anything, our need for traditional knowledge becomes
> ever more acute as we strain the planet's carrying capacity.
> (2007: 15)

Further Reading

Aissen, J. 2007. Saving endangered languages. http://review.ucsc.edu/
fal107/Rev_F07_pp14–15_EndangeredLanguages.pdf (accessed
March 15, 2009).

Brown, C. 1984. *Languages and living things: Uniformities in folk classification and naming.* New Brunswick, N.J.: Rutgers University Press.

Chung, S. 2008. How much can understudied languages really tell us about how languages work? Invited plenary lecture, Annual Meeting of the Linguistic Society of America. http://people.ucsc. edu/ schung/chung_lsa2008.pdf (accessed March 15, 2009).

Corbett, G. 2001. Why linguists need languages. In L. Maffi, ed., *On biocultural diversity: Linking language, knowledge, and the environment,* 82–94. Washington, D.C.: Smithsonian Institution Press.

Crystal, D. 2000. *Language death.* New York: Cambridge University Press.

Danzinger, E. 2005. The eye of the beholder: How linguistic categorization affects "natural" experience. In S. McKinnon and S. Silverman, eds., *Complexities: Beyond nature and nurture,* 64–80. Chicago: University of Chicago Press.

Dixon, R. 1997. *The rise and fall of languages.* New York: Cambridge University Press.

Dorian, N. 2002. Commentary: Broadening the rhetorical and descriptive horizons in endangered language linguistics. *Journal of Linguistic Anthropology* 12(2): 134–40.

Errington, J. 2003. Getting language rights: The rhetoric of language endangerment and loss. *American Anthropologist* 105(4): 723–32.

Fillmore, L. 1999. When learning a second language means losing the first. *Early Childhood Research Quarterly* 6: 323–46.

Fishman, J. 1982. Whorfianism of the third kind: Ethnolinguistic diversity as a worldwide societal asset. *Language in Society* 11: 1–14.

Gordon, R., ed. 2005. *Ethnologue: Languages of the world.* Dallas: SIL International.

Grenoble, L., and L. Whaley. 2006. *Saving languages: An introduction to language revitalization.* New York: Cambridge University Press.

Grimes, B., ed. 2000. Ethnology: Languages of the world, 14th edition. Dallas: Summer Institute of Linguistics. http://www.ethnologue.com (accessed March 15, 2009).

Harrison, K. D. 2007. *When languages die*. New York: Oxford University Press.

Haspelmath, M., M. Dryer, D. Gil, and B. Comrie, eds. 2005. *The world atlas of language structures*. New York: Oxford University Press.

Hill, J. 2002. "Expert rhetorics" in advocacy of endangered languages: Who is listening and what do they hear? *Journal of Linguistic Anthropology* 12(2): 119–33.

Hinton, L. 2001. The use of linguistic archives in language revitalization. In L. Hinton and K. Hale, eds., *The green book of language revitalization in practice*, 419–23. San Diego: Academic Press.

Krauss, M. 1991. The world's languages in crisis. *Language* 68(1): 4–10.

Ladefoged, P. 1992. Another view of endangered languages. *Language* 68(4): 809–11.

Living Tongues Institute for Endangered Languages. http://www.livingtongues.org (accessed March 2009).

Nettle, D., and S. Romaine. 2000. *Vanishing voices: The extinction of the world's languages*. New York: Oxford University Press.

Nonaka, A. 2004. Sign languages: The forgotten endangered languages: Lessons on the importance of remembering. *Language in Society* 33(05): 737–67.

Oozeva, C., C. Noongwook, G. Noongwook, C. Alowa, and I. Krupnik. 2004. *Watching ice and weather our way* / Akulki, Tapghaghmii, Mangtaaquli, Sunqaanga, Igor Krupnik. *Sikumengllu eslamengllu esghapallenghput*, ed. I. Krupnik, H. Huntington, C. Koonooka, and G. Noongwook. Washington, D.C.: Arctic Studies Center, Smithsonian Institution.

Shaw, P. 2001. Language and identity, language and the land. *British Columbia Studies* 131: 39–55.

Sutherland, W. 2003. Parallel extinction risk and global distribution of languages and species. *Nature* 423: 276–79.

Whalen, D. 2004. How the study of endangered languages will revolutionize linguistics. In Piet van Sterkenberg, ed., *Linguistics today: Facing a greater challenge*, 321–42. Amsterdam: Benjamins.

Keywords

language death
language endangerment
understudied languages

Index

CPSIA information can be obtained
at www.ICGtesting.com
Printed in the USA
BVOW04s2214261116
468934BV00001B/4/P